Solar Remodeling In Northern New Mexico
Edited by Michael Shepard
New Mexico Solar Energy Association
P.O. Box 2004
(1372½ Cerrillos Road—505-983-2861)
Santa Fe, NM 87501

First Printing 1981

This guide was prepared with assistance from Oregon Appropriate Technology, a solar energy consulting group, and Western Solar Utilization Network, a contractor to the U.S. Department of Energy. Western SUN increases the public awareness and commercialization of solar energy in Alaska, Arizona, California, Colorado, Hawaii, Idaho, Montana, Nevada, New Mexico, Oregon, Utah, Washington, and Wyoming.

Contributors:

Don Corson	Susan Degen
Sam Sadler	Don Williams
Phillip Johnson	Rachel Snyder
M. Steven Baker	Ron Pogue
David Edrington	Aileen Jeffries
Rob Thallon	Michael Shepard
A. Lee Gilbert	Cliff Terry
Mark Gorrell, Illustrator	Alex Wilson

LEGAL NOTICE:

ABOUT THE NEW MEXICO SOLAR ENERGY ASSOCIATION

The New Mexico Solar Energy Association is one of the world's leading solar organizations. Founded by a handful of solar pioneers in the early 1970's, the NMSEA is a non-profit, membership-supported group dedicated to furthering solar and related arts. Its 2500 members hail from all fifty states and over forty foreign countries.

From it's main offices in Santa Fe and through local affiliate groups throughout New Mexico, the Association educates the public on all facets of the solar field. A $15 tax deductible membership in the NMSEA includes a subscription to the Association's acclaimed monthly journal, the SUNPAPER, and discounts on solar design assistance, informative conferences and workshops, and other NMSEA publications.

An extensive solar library at the Association's offices offers free access to solar home plans, reference works on all facets of alternative energy, solar product literature, and a wide selection of periodicals.

If you would like to learn more about solar energy, need help in designing your solar addition, or just want to support a good cause, join the NMSEA today. Your $15 membership will keep you abreast of the latest developments in the field and will support the Association's efforts in furthering a solar fueled future. To join, or to find out more about the NMSEA, fill out the handy form below.

☐ Please enroll me in the NMSEA. Enclosed is my check for $15.
☐ Please send a sample copy of the SUNPAPER. Enclosed is my check for $2.
☐ Please send further information on the NMSEA. Enclosed is 50¢ for postage and handling.

Name _____

Address _____

City_____ State_____ Zip_____

Make checks payable to NMSEA, P.O. Box 2004, Santa Fe, NM 87501 (505) 983-2861.

ACKNOWLEDGEMENTS

I would like to thank the good people at Oregon Appropriate Technology and my friends Rachel Snyder, Ron Pogue, Aileen Jeffries, Maggie Kuhn and Cliff Terry for their work in the development of this guide. Special thanks to Alex Wilson, Jane Marx, and the rest of the NMSEA staff for their help in preparing portions of the guide specific to Northern New Mexico. And to the New Mexico Energy and Minerals Department, many thanks for providing printing funds.

Michael Shepard

USING THE GUIDE

This guide isn't meant to be read from cover to cover. Some chapters will be appropriate for your needs, others you needn't bother to read. The flow chart on the next two pages will help you to use the guide efficiently. Black tabs on the margins of pages throughout the text correspond to the topics listed at the right side of the flow chart. For example, to find out about securing a loan for your solar installation turn to those pages in the text which have a black tab along the margin at the same level as the "Finances" key on the right side of the flow chart.

Using Solar Energy

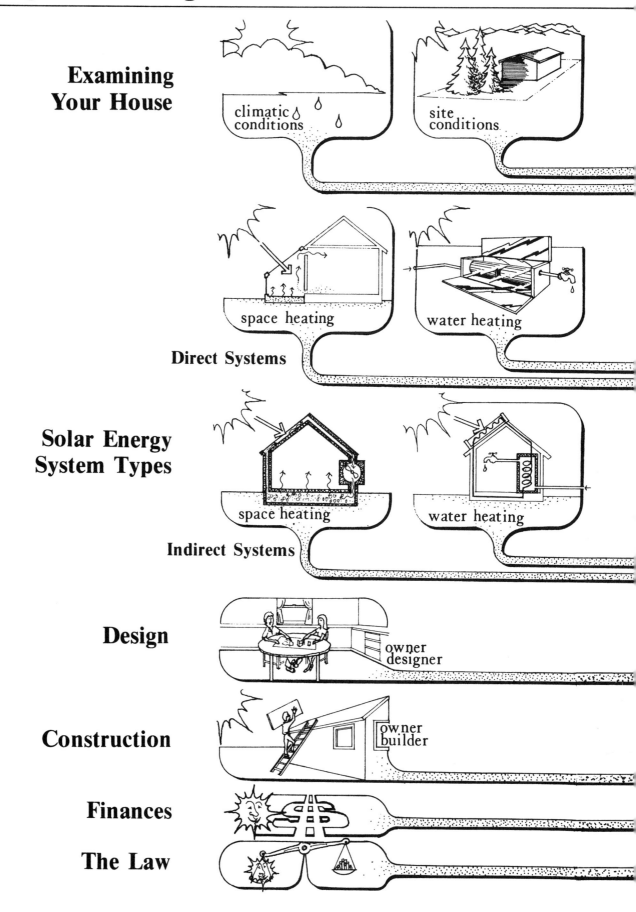

Examining Your House

climatic conditions

site conditions

Direct Systems

space heating

water heating

Solar Energy System Types

space heating

water heating

Indirect Systems

Design

owner designer

Construction

owner builder

Finances

The Law

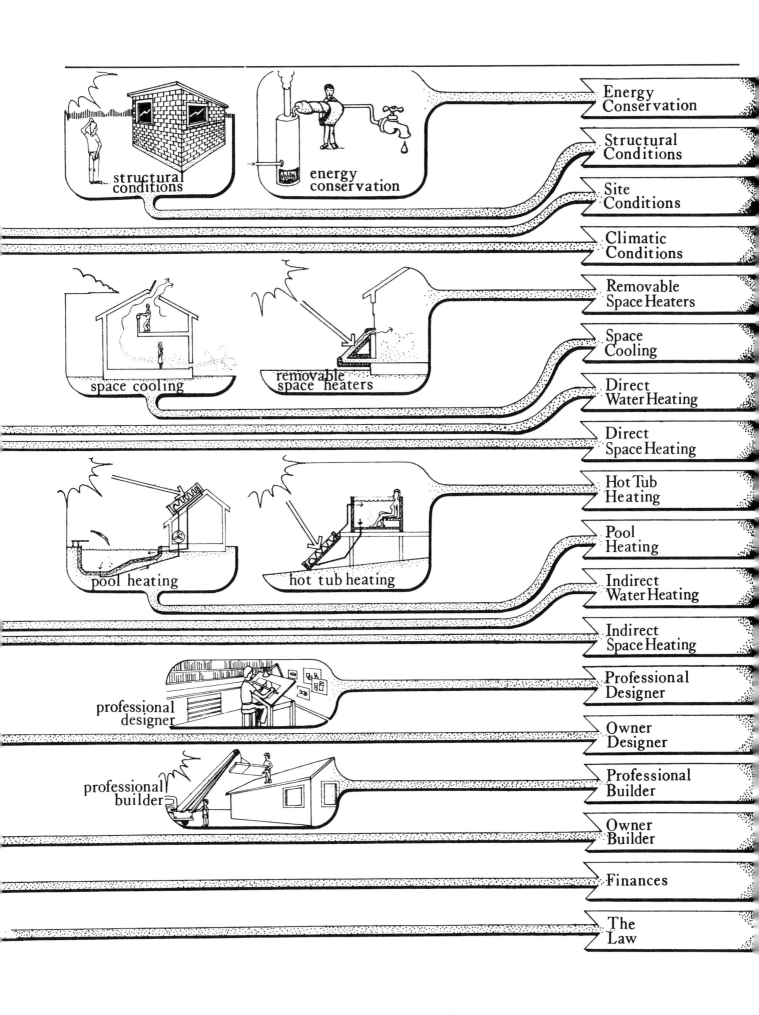

Energy
Conservation

Structural
Conditions

Site
Conditions

Climatic
Conditions

Removable
Space Heaters

Space
Cooling

Direct
Water Heating

Direct
Space Heating

Hot Tub
Heating

Pool
Heating

Indirect
Water Heating

Indirect
Space Heating

Professional
Designer

Owner
Designer

Professional
Builder

Owner
Builder

Finances

The
Law

structural
conditions

energy
conservation

space cooling

removable
space heaters

pool heating

hot tub heating

professional
designer

professional
builder

CONTENTS

WHAT THIS GUIDE CAN DO FOR YOU

This guide is for homeowners—like you—who are interested in using solar energy in their present homes.

For many homeowners interested in finding out whether the sun can begin to work for them *now*, the problem isn't too little information, but too much. Walk into virtually any bookstore these days, and you'll be confronted with shelves of books on solar energy. How can you sort through the dozens of brightly colored, promising books to find the information you really need?

This guide will help you to deal with the problem. It isn't intended to be another solar energy book, but rather a guide to steer you by the simplest and most direct route to the answers to some basic questions:

- Will solar energy work for my present home?
- What method would be most effective?
- How much will it cost?
- Can and should I build it myself?
- What can I expect in dealing with designers and contractors?

This guide won't tell you how to design or install a solar collector. It doesn't include detailed information on all the different possibilities for solar improvements, nor does it discuss new solar homes. Instead, it will help you make a solid, confident decision about your basic options. It will help you finance your investment and help you claim your tax credits. It will also help prepare you to deal with designers, contractors, and building officials so that you can get what you really want at a price you can afford.

> A note to the reader: Terms which may be new to you are *italicized* when they are first used. These words are defined in the glossary found in the back of the guide.

The sun is our oldest and most familiar resource. We have relied on the sun for centuries, and it has only been during the past century that we have ignored the sun in our brief fling with exhaustible fossil fuels.

The abundance of this resource is staggering. The world around, the amount of solar energy falling on the average rooftop is enough to provide 10 times the heating needs of those dwelling within, if all this energy could be harnessed.

Sadly, our use of this energy is being hampered by the common misconception that tapping the sun's resources requires exotic, unproven technologies. It does not. Solar energy is a natural, direct source of heat which is easily used.

Peoples the world over have known for thousands of years how to build structures to receive the maximum amount of winter sunlight and summer shade. The Greeks began designing homes and even entire cities for maximum access to winter sunlight some 2500 years ago. The world's first community planned for using the sun was probably Olynthus, built in the 5th century B.C. All houses faced south, guaranteeing access to sunlight for rich and poor alike. Main rooms opened onto south-facing porches which let in the sun during the winter and excluded it in the summer, while virtually windowless north walls provided a defense against the wind.

The Greeks were not alone. Similar developments took place in China at about the same time. The Romans used the sun to heat their famous baths, warmed their homes with solar heated greenhouses, and codified the first law stipulating the right to sunlight. Building with the sun was also a familiar practice in the ancient Americas; the entire Meso-American city of Teotihuacan was laid out on a grid facing south, and the Anasazi Indians were building pueblos in the 11th century that strikingly resembled Olynthus.

The Dark Ages were dark for solar energy as well, but by the 17th century the *solar greenhouse* had been rediscovered, and for the next two centuries this device was steadily improved in England and on the Continent. The sophisticated use of greenhouses and conservatories for both horticulture and heating became common, going out of fashion only with the advent of cheap fossil fuels.

Solar water heaters came into vogue in Southern California in the 1890s, and tens of thousands were sold in a boom that lasted through the 1920s, when natural gas

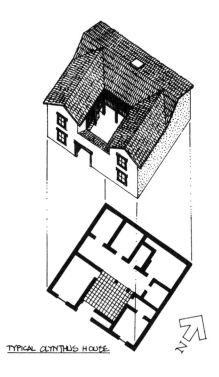

TYPICAL OLYNTHUS HOUSE

Opposite Page: Sun tempered Anasazi Indian ruins at Mesa Verde, Colorado illustrate ancient understanding of solar principles. The cliff overhang shades in summer and blocks cold northern winter winds. The low winter sun warms the caves by penetrating under the cliff overhang and striking the back walls.

became so cheap that solar energy couldn't compete. After World War II there was a veritable solar craze, as popular magazines trumpeted the energy savings possible for homes that made intelligent use of the sun. Only in the '50s, as the war-time conservation ethic faded and fuels became cheaper, did the use of solar energy go into dormancy once again.

Sweeping predictions have been made for solar energy's long-range potential. It has been estimated that we can make a complete 'solar transition' within 50 years, ultimately supplying all our energy through use of the sun. A substantial portion of this solar transition has already begun. Many quite simple solar approaches are tested and available for home use; these simple methods are already being used in roughly 200,000 American homes, schools, and businesses. Not every method will work for every house, but almost every house has some potential for using the sun.

It is estimated that household energy costs will increase by about 15 to 20 per cent annually during the coming decade; little more need be said about the common-sense value of using the sun to cut household energy bills. A solar energy improvement can be a good investment, enhancing the value of your house.

Even before thinking of solar heating or cooling improvements, though, you should take advantage of another opportunity: conservation. Solar energy can be far more effective and meet a far greater percentage of a house's needs if energy use has been reduced to a minimum. No new energy source is as cost-effective as conservation.

Once all conservation measures have been taken, it is time to begin making decisions about adding solar improvements to your home. The constraints are greater in *retrofitting*—adding solar improvements to existing homes—than for designing new homes. But if we as a society are to begin reaping the benefits of solar energy before several generations have passed, it is essential that the challenge of improving existing houses be met today.

There is a popular misconception that the cost of solar equipment will come down in a few years through the efficiencies of mass production. In reality, most solar systems use fairly standard plumbing, air conditioning, and building materials, and it isn't likely that the costs of lumber, copper, and insulation will be getting any lower.

There is also an understandable concern that solar systems may still have a lot of 'bugs' to be worked out or that there may be dramatic breakthroughs in the near future. This might be true of some of the more innovative approaches now being tested. However, the typical solar home improvement will involve such things as solar water heaters and greenhouses, and, as we have seen, these methods are anything but new or untried.

There are strong personal satisfactions as well as economic advantages to be gained from using the sun's heat. There is a sense of greater self-reliance and peace of mind that comes with using your own home to meet your energy needs, thereby reducing your dependence on external suppliers.

Use of solar energy is simply intelligent husbandry of one's resources. It involves an awareness of your house's orientation, the sun's shifting position in the sky over the year, the general climate of the region, the weather that affects your particular location, and the seasonal changes in vegetation. When you live in a solar home, these things aren't simply part of the external environment, but become an active part of your life.

The promise of solar energy is great, but to partake of it, the individual homeowner will have to take the initiative. It is up to you to decide which solar improvements, if any, are appropriate for your house, and to plan what course of action is best for you to take. The purpose of this guide is to help you make these decisions.

You probably are already familiar with basic solar concepts. In case you aren't, here is a brief refresher to get you started. Specific applications will be treated in more detail in Chapter 4.

HEAT: THE SOLAR BUILDING BLOCK

Sunlight and heat follow a number of basic rules.

When sunlight strikes an object, it is either *reflected* (as off a mirror), *transmitted* (as through a window), or *absorbed* (as by black pavement).

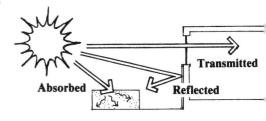

Light from the sun turns to heat when absorbed by objects it strikes. Sunlight streaming through a window turns to heat after being absorbed by walls, floors, and furniture, which store this heat and later release it.

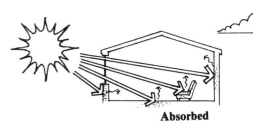

Heat will always travel from a warm place to a cooler place. Insulating your house helps to slow this movement down, keeping more of your precious heat inside in the winter. During summer months, insulation helps keep hot air from moving to your cooler inside areas.

Some materials can store more heat than others and retain it for a longer period of time. Heavy materials like water and stone are good for storing heat from the sun.

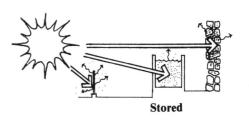

Heat travels in three ways. When heat travels through solid objects, it is known as *conduction*.

Heat carried by moving air or water currents is called *convection*. Warm air or warm water naturally rises while cooler air or water naturally sinks.

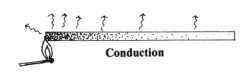

Warm objects give off heat directly as *radiation*.

PUTTING SOLAR ENERGY TO WORK

Solar energy can fill many needs in the home. This guide covers four of the most common applications.

- Water heating for kitchen, laundry, and bath
- Heating for your house in winter
- Cooling for your house in summer
- Water heating for swimming pool or hot tub

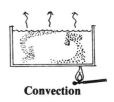

In considering your solar options, you will find the terms *active* and *passive* used to describe various approaches to solar energy use.

Active approaches are typified by solar collectors on a roof, wall, or lawn. Active devices use electric pumps or fans to move solar heated air or water from where it's collected to where it's stored to where you need it.

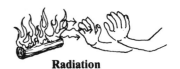

Passive approaches generally work without electricity, relying instead on a house's windows, walls, or floors to collect and store solar energy. When needed, the heat is released and moved naturally.

6

Passive and active systems are not mutually exclusive. Elements of each can be combined to form the most appropriate solar improvement.

SOLAR HEATED WATER FOR KITCHEN, BATH, AND LAUNDRY

Systems for producing hot water for home use generally rely on solar collectors, a separate *heat storage* tank, and a piping system to distribute the water.

Some systems use pumps to circulate the water, while others rely on natural convection.

Another type of system, known as a *batch water heater*, uses the storage tank as the collector.

SOLAR HEATING FOR YOUR HOUSE

There are several approaches to heating your home with solar energy.

Direct Gain

In a *direct gain* approach, the living space is heated directly by the sun. Sunlight entering through south-facing windows, skylights, *clerestories*, or sliding glass doors is absorbed and stored by *thermal mass* in the rooms.

Solar Greenhouses

Attached solar greenhouses include enough thermal mass (water in containers or masonry) to absorb sunlight entering through south-facing glass and store its heat. This heat can be moved to the rest of the house either by vents and fans, or through a mass wall where the greenhouse joins the house.

Thermal Storage Walls

Thermal storage walls stand behind south-facing glass. Made of heavy masonry—usually concrete, brick, or adobe—or containers filled with water, they absorb heat and then release it slowly and steadily to the interior.

Wall Collectors

Daytime house heating can be provided by collectors installed onto walls or *window boxes* attached to existing windows. These collectors are used to heat air which then can rise naturally or be blown into the room; cooler air from the inside is drawn into the collector through natural convection. These systems usually only provide heat during the day, since most don't include heat storage.

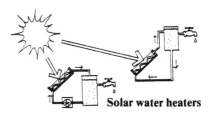
Solar water heaters

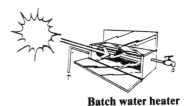
Batch water heater

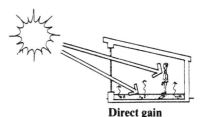
Direct gain

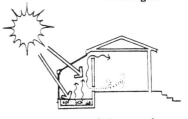
Solar greenhouse

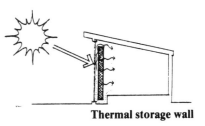
Thermal storage wall

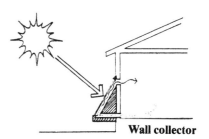
Wall collector

Air Collector Systems

In *air collector systems* air is blown through a collector which consists of an insulated box covered by *glazing* and containing a blackened absorber surface. This heated surface warms the air, which can then be blown through a storage medium, usually a bed of rocks, where the heat is transferred to the storage material. The air then continues around the loop back to the collector or is sent to the house.

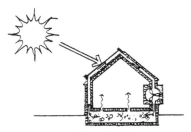
Air collection system

Liquid Collector Systems

Some systems use liquid instead of air. Liquid either trickles across a blackened surface *(trickle collector)* or runs through a series of tubes in the collector *(flat plate collector)*. It is then piped to a storage tank. This heat can be used in the house by pumping the warm liquid through pipes in the floor or in baseboard heaters, or by pumping air past the heated liquid as part of a forced-air system.

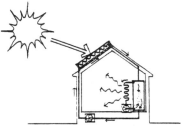
Liquid collection system

NATURAL COOLING FOR YOUR HOUSE

Thermal Mass

You can use natural air flows to cool as well as to heat your house. For instance, instead of storing solar heat absorbed from sunlight during the day for later use at night, mass such as masonry or water can be used to absorb unwanted heat from the interior during the day and release it to the outside during the cooler evening hours.

Cooling with thermal mass

Shading

Shading is an important part of natural cooling. Overhangs or portable screens can be positioned to block the sun's rays during the summer, when the sun is high in the sky, while admitting sunlight during the winter, when the sun is lower on the horizon. Deciduous (leafy) trees and vines can sometimes be planted where they will block sunlight during the summer.

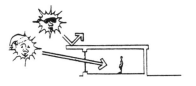
Cooling with shading

Natural Ventilation

A great deal of cooling can be provided through proper ventilation. Vents should be placed high so that warm air escapes from the top of rooms or the attic, while cool air enters through lower openings. Windows should be placed to allow for cooling winds to flow through the house.

Cooling with natural ventilation

HEATING YOUR SWIMMING POOL OR HOT TUB

Pool

Pool heating is one of the most effective uses of solar energy. The pool itself serves as storage medium, and since relatively low temperatures are involved, simple collectors can be used. A pool cover prevents heat from escaping when the pool is not being used. Clear pool covers can actually serve as simple solar heaters, raising pool temperatures five to ten degrees by admitting sunlight and trapping heat.

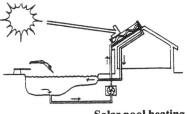

Solar pool heating

Hot Tub

Hot tubs require somewhat more effective collectors than pools, since higher temperatures are involved, but still represent prime opportunities to reduce energy bills through use of the sun.

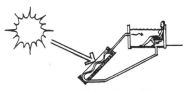

Solar hot tub heating

This has been only a brief refresher of solar concepts and approaches available to you. Many of these techniques can be combined, depending upon what is most appropriate for your house and needs.

RESOURCES

Sunset Homeowner's Guide to Solar Heating, by the Editors of Sunset Books and Sunset Magazines, Menlo Park, California (Lane Publishing Company, second printing, 1979).

The Solar Home Book, by Bruce Anderson (Cheshire Books, Harrisville, NH, 1976).

Sunpaper: Bulletin of the New Mexico Solar Energy Association, $15/year from the NMSEA, P.O. Box 2004, Santa Fe, NM (505) 983-2861.

SOLAR ENERGY IN NORTHERN NEW MEXICO

Northern New Mexico is very sunny. It also has cold winters which make the cost of home heating a major burden for many local homeowners. These two factors—lots of sun and plenty of cold weather, make this an ideal area for solar energy use.

Many homes in Northern New Mexico are not insulated, and with energy costs rising here just as they are everywhere else, these homes cost a great deal to heat. Annual space and water heating bills of $1000 are common throughout the region. With fuel costs escalating as they are, many conventional homes could have utility bills of two, three, or four times this amount within a decade.

Because of rising energy costs and other factors such as concern for the environment, many of your neighbors have already turned to the sun for their energy needs. From Albuquerque to Taos, from Las Vegas to Chama, several thousand solar water heating and space heating and cooling systems are in place already, and the number is growing daily.

Just about any kind of solar heating or cooling system will work here. And just about any existing house in the region whatever its design, can be modified to take some advantage of the sun's free energy. Fortunately, the predominant one story flat-roofed adobe style is particularly adaptable to low cost solar remodeling.

South facing adobe or block walls can be turned into solar heaters simply by painting them a dark color and attaching glass or plastic to the outside. The massive structure of most homes in the area is ideal for storing heat collected by greenhouses, skylights, windows, thermal storage walls, and other "passive" systems described in Chapter 2. This mass also helps with summer cooling by absorbing heat from the air. Water heating is easy too as the scarcity of shade casting trees and the predominance of flat roofs makes for very easy installation of these systems.

The suitability of the prevailing architecture to solar applications and the sunny climate open a whole range of possibilities. The photographs which follow show a few of the many systems which are already hard at work providing energy to local homes. They also demonstrate that whether you are rich or poor, live in a big house or a small one, there's a way that you can use the sun to save money, save energy, beautify your home, and help preserve the environment.

This skylight has a reflector which bounces the low winter rays into the room below. In summer the reflector can be covered to shade the skylight. A black metal tank mounted under the glazing serves as a batch water heater. An installation of this kind can be done for several hundred dollars — less if recycled materials are used.

These flat plate collectors are part of an active domestic hot water heating system. Including pumps, thermostats, storage tank and controls, commercially purchased systems range from $1500 to $3500. Tax credits can cut the actual cost by over 60%.

Greenhouses are probably the most popular solar addition. They provide pleasant living space, heat, and an opportunity for year round gardening. They can be an elegant custom addition or a simple but functional home built space. This greenhouse, designed by Valerie Walsh, features curved laminated mahogany beams and a hot tub. Custom work of this quality costs at least fifty dollars per square foot.

Home built greenhouse like this one can heat themselves and an adjacent area up to twice their size while costing five to ten dollars per square foot of floor area in materials. Remember that tax credits can return a sizable portion of any investment in solar devices.

Clerestories can provide light and heat to spaces on the north end of a house.

Next page, top: These owner built clerestories cost well under a thousand dollars and provide heating for this uninsulated artist's studio in Santa Fe.

Next page, bottom: This attractive direct gain space stores heat in brick floors and massive walls. Existing houses can easily be remodeled using these principles by adding windows on the south side, an overhang for summer shading, and thermal mass for heat storage. Costs range widely depending on the kind of glazing that is used, whether adequate mass is already present, and other factors.

A thermal storage wall provides gentle radiant heat. It can be quite attractive, or, as in the example on the next page, simple, cheap and functional.

A well designed solar application is geared specifically
to the local climate. The following climatic data for Northern
New Mexico will help you when you get to the design stage
in sizing and orienting your solar addition. Some of the
numbers may be confusing at first. Don't let them scare you;
any solar designer can help you to understand them.

CLIMATIC DATA FOR
NORTHERN
NEW MEXICO

MONTHLY AND ANNUAL MEAN TEMPERATURES (1)

	J	F	M	A	M	J	J	A	S	O	N	D	Year
Albuquerque	35	40	46	56	65	75	79	77	70	58	45	36	57
Santa Fe	30	34	38	48	57	66	70	68	62	52	39	31	50
Farmington	29	35	41	50	60	68	75	73	65	53	45	39	54

MONTHLY AND ANNUAL MEAN HEATING DEGREE DAYS

Heating degree days are the number of degrees the daily average temperature is below 65° F.

	J	F	M	A	M	J	J	A	S	O	N	D	Year
Albuquerque	924	700	595	282	58	0	0	0	7	218	615	893	4292
Santa Fe	1091	882	828	513	258	68	5	21	116	409	774	1042	6009
Farmington	1128	840	756	465	184	36	0	6	67	375	774	1082	5713

WINTER DESIGN TEMPERATURE (1)

This is the reference temperature used for sizing the capacity of the conventional heating system of a house. The average outside temperature drops below this value less than 2.5% of the time.

Albuquerque 17° F   **Santa Fe** 9° F   **Farmington** 9° F

AVERAGE DAILY TOTAL RADIATION AVAILABLE TO FIXED COLLECTORS OF DIFFERENT TILTS FACING TRUE NORTH

The values are given in BTUs/ft^2 day. They are based upon data recorded in Albuquerque. Values for other locations in New Mexico will be generally within 10% of these. Larger differences may exist for locations which are in the shaded area of the map. These values are average values. On particular days the actual value may be as low as 20% of these or they may be 20 or 25% more than these numbers depending on whether that day is exceptionally cloudy or especially clear.

Collector Tilt above horizontal	J	F	M	A	M	J	J	A	S	O	N	D
0	1050	1300	1710	2250	2540	2570	2440	2280	1870	1550	1140	920
15	1400	1590	2060	2380	2510	2540	2470	2320	2060	1840	1470	1240
30	1590	1780	2090	2350	2380	2320	2280	2280	2130	2000	1710	1460
45	1740	1840	2090	2160	2090	2030	2030	2060	2060	2030	1870	1650
60	1810	1810	1970	1900	1780	1620	1650	1740	1870	2000	1870	1680
75	1710	1710	1710	1550	1360	1140	1240	1360	1590	1810	1780	1650
90	1550	1490	1360	1140	860	700	790	920	1170	1550	1590	1490

MEAN PERCENTAGE OF POSSIBLE SUNSHINE (2)

Data are available only for Albuquerque. For other locations, except for the shaded mountainous areas on the map, actual values will be within a few percentage points around these data.

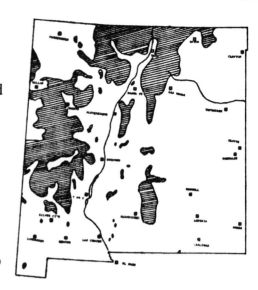

J	F	M	A	M	J	J
70	72	72	76	79	84	76

A	S	O	N	D	Year
76	81	80	79	70	76

PREVAILING DIRECTION AND MEAN SPEED OF WIND

Data available only for Albuquerque. (2)

	J	F	M	A	M	J	J	A	S	O	N	D
Prevailing direction	N	N	SE	SE	S	SE	SE	SE	SE	SE	N	N
Mean Speed	8	9	10	11	10	10	9	8	9	8	8	7

SUN ANGLES (4)

Values for 36° NL. Time is solar time. Altitude angle

Month/Time	am:	5	6	7	8	9	10	11	12
	pm:	7	6	5	4	3	2	1	
Dec. 21					8	16	23	28	30
Jan. 21/Nov. 21				0	10	20	27	32	34
Feb. 21/Oct. 21				5	16	26	35	40	43
Mar. 21/Sept. 21			0	12	23	34	44	51	53
Apr. 21/Aug. 21			7	19	30	42	53	62	65
May 21/July 21		0	11	23	35	47	58	69	74
June 21		3	14	25	37	49	61	72	78

*Azimuth angle time	am:	5	6	7	8	9	10	11	12
	pm:	7	6	5	4	3	2	1	12
Dec. 21					53	42	30	16	0
Jan. 21/Nov. 21				65	50	45	33	17	0
Feb. 21/Oct. 21				72	63	52	38	20	0
Mar. 21/Sept. 21			90	81	70	60	45	25	0
Apr. 21/Aug. 21			99	91	81	70	55	34	0
May 21/ July 21		115	106	98	90	81	67	44	0
June 21		117	109	102	95	80	72	51	0

REFERENCES

(1) Energy conservation code, NMEI, The University of New Mexico.
(2) Climatic Atlas of the United States, U.S. Department of Commerce.
(3) The New Mexico Solar Energy Resource, Raymond J. Bahm, University of New Mexico
(4) The Passive Solar Energy Book, Edward Mazria.

CHAPTER 4

YOUR HOUSE AND THE SUN

You've just had a brief introduction to solar energy, your climate, and your solar options. Now we come to the crux of the matter: your decision as to whether solar energy can be useful to you and, if so, what kind of solar improvement would be most appropriate for your house.

You're ready to start working toward your solar decision. The rest of this chapter will help you to

- Evaluate your site for its solar potential
- Examine your house to see how it affects your options

Think of this chapter as a tool kit for decision-making. First, you'll learn the different considerations and how they relate to each other. Then we'll help you look at various aspects of your house to see how they affect your solar options. You should then know enough to make a preliminary decision about your ability to use the sun.

Since your purpose here is to arrive at a basic decision, not to work out the exact details, you will proceed through a series of topics dealing with parts of your house and yard. Each topic will include recommendations intended to steer you toward the likeliest possibilities.

When you have finished this chapter you should have a good idea of which solar options make the most sense for your house. If an option seems promising, a number set off in the margin will direct you to the relevant part of Chapter 5. If you see a particular number appearing frequently next to the material that seems to apply to your house, consider this a likely option and go to Chapter 5 to read about it in more detail.

The first step, however, even before you begin to think about heating or cooling with the sun, is to realize your potential energy savings through conservation. Not only is conservation cheaper than any new source of energy, but any solar system you may eventually choose to install will be more efficient and thus more cost-effective if you have already plugged your house's "energy leaks."

RECOMMENDATION

You should examine your house for energy leaks, and take every possible step to achieve energy savings through conservation, before making any decision about using solar energy.

For more information on energy conservation and how to arrange a home energy analysis, see the Appendix.

YOUR SITE'S MICROCLIMATE

Your lot has its own unique characteristics, known as its *microclimate*. A microclimate is created by the conditions of your immediate vicinity: topography and vegetation and the ways in which wind and sun interact with them. In most cases, your microclimate won't differ drastically from generalized local conditions. But there can be significant exceptions.

In some cases, you can modify your microclimate. You might be able to provide summer shading by planting deciduous trees. You may also be able to block or change the direction of the wind by planting trees or locating structures or fences in strategic spots. In other cases, you will have to accept the disadvantages of your microclimate.

Take a day or so and look at the general characteristics of your neighborhood. Take note of the heights and locations of buildings and trees, the location of hills, and wind patterns.

If heating is a primary concern, look next at the amount of sunlight that falls on your lot. Remember that during the winter months the sun is low in the southern sky; while it can easily pass under moderate overhangs during this period, it can also be easily blocked by adjacent buildings, hills, and trees many yards away. If you look during December or January you can make a rough estimate of your access to sunlight by direct observation. But at another time of year you may not be sure from direct observation of how much sunlight falls on your lot, and you may want to plot the shading pattern on the *sun chart* found in the Appendix.

You need direct sunlight striking your house or its immediate vicinity between about 9 a.m. and 3 p.m. on a day in December or January. However, the exact hours aren't too important. The more sunlight you receive, the better are your possibilities for using solar energy.

If you find it too difficult to do this preliminary analysis yourself, consider consulting a solar designer for assistance.

If cooling is your primary interest, the usable amount of sunlight falling on your house won't be so important. Instead, you will examine your house for opportunities to provide shading during summer months and catch summer breezes. In this case, you can use the sun chart to determine sun angles for designing shading devices.

Using the sun to help heat pools or hot tubs is fairly straightforward. Use the sun chart to determine the amount of sunlight falling on your yard (if necessary), and then turn directly to the sections on pools and hot tub heating in Chapter 5.

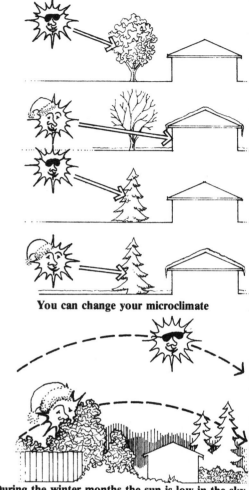

You can change your microclimate

During the winter months the sun is low in the sky.

(4, 5)

20

THE SUN CHART

Take a close look around your house. You may find from direct observation that you have good exposure to sunlight year-round on your roof, south walls, or in your yard next to the house. Remember as you look that the winter sun is quite low in the sky and can be blocked by objects. Follow the path of the sun across the horizon from east to west, and if it is clear that you have good access, then you can skip the sun chart.

If your access to sun at these likely-looking spots is not clear or if it is partially shaded during part of the year, then you should use the sun chart found at the end of the book to determine the amount of sunlight available.

The sun chart plots the sun's path across the sky. The horizontal lines represent the sun's altitude above the horizon in degrees. You can clearly see how the sun is lower in the sky in the winter. The vertical lines represent the *bearing angle,* or the position of the sun measured to the east or west of true south. The heavy solid lines are the paths of the sun on the 20th of each month, and the dashed lines represent time of day. Using the chart, you can locate the position of the sun in the sky at any time during any day of the year. You can also determine the times that direct sunlight is blocked from your site by plotting the skyline directly on the sun chart.

To plot the skyline you will need a compass or a *transit* to find the bearing angles, a hand level to find the *solar altitude* angles, and a copy of the sun chart.

If you can't borrow a hand level or transit, take page 106 and glue it to a piece of stiff cardboard. Place a pin with a weighted thread in the pin hole and bring someone with you to read the angle of altitude while you sight the horizon along the top edge of the cardboard.

Place yourself at the location you have selected and plot the skyline from that point on a copy of the sun chart as follows:

1. Using the compass or transit, determine the direction of true south, remembering that true south in Northern New Mexico is about 11½° east of magnetic south, which the compass reads.

2. Aim the hand level or transit toward true south and determine the altitude (angle above the horizon) of the skyline (the highest point that casts a shadow). Plot this on the sun chart above the bearing angle 0°.

3. Similarly, determine and record the altitude of the skyline for each 15° along the horizon both to the east and west of south continuing to the edge of the chart. Then connect the points you've plotted.

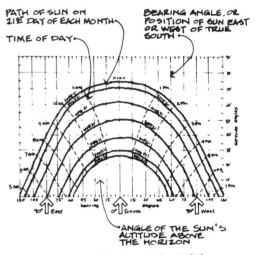

LINES ON THE SUN CHART

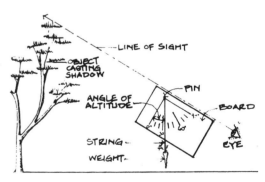

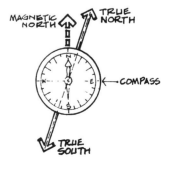

4. For isolated tall objects such as evergreen trees and buildings, find both bearing angles and altitude individually and plot them.
5. Finally, plot in deciduous trees and outline them with dots on the chart.

The areas above the solid line on the chart represent the times when the sun will reach your selected point on your site. The areas below the line represent the times when that location will be shaded. The areas below the dotted line represent the times when that location will be shaded when the deciduous trees have their leaves.

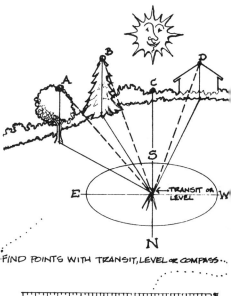

...FIND POINTS WITH TRANSIT, LEVEL or COMPASS...

...PLOT POINTS ON SUN CHART AND CONNECT

RECOMMENDATION

In general, you need access to sunlight from 9 a.m. to 3 p.m. during the winter.

According to rough rules of thumb, you will need a sunny area of about 10 to 20 square feet (sq. ft.) for each person in your house to provide most of the hot water they need.

To provide substantial space heating assistance, use the following rules of thumb:

Direct Gain Windows	The glass area should be 11% to 25% of the size of the heated floor area.
Solar Greenhouse	The glass area should be 33% to 90% of the size of the heated floor area of the house.
Thermal Storage Wall	The glass area should be 40% to 100% of the size of the heated floor area.
Active System	The glass area should be 40% to 60% of the size of the heated floor area.

Check these rules of thumb for your house and family to see how much solar access you need and compare this with your sun chart.

If you have a swimming pool or hot tub and any direct sunlight falls on your site during the months you need water heating for these uses, you should consider using the sun. (4,5)

For cooling, examine your site for opportunities to provide shading and to direct summer breezes toward your house.

EXAMINING YOUR HOUSE

You should now have a rough idea of your site's solar potential. A solar option may be technically feasible for your site, and yet difficulties may arise when you attempt to add it to your house. The time has come to examine your house to see how well various solar options might fit with its structure, or how easily they might be incorporated into an addition.

To do this you need to consider your house:

    A.   Basic shape and orientation
    B.   Floor plan
    C.   South walls and windows
    D.   Roof
    E.   Structural characteristics
    F.   Heat storage possibilities
    G.   Existing mechanical systems
    H.   Other remodeling possibilities

Studying your house will help you to understand the types of solar improvements that might be appropriate for your house. Take your time, and think through each item.

A. BASIC SHAPE AND ORIENTATION

The basic shape and orientation of your house are important when considering using solar energy. The south side of your house receives nearly three times more solar energy in the winter than the east and west sides. If you have large areas of unshaded south walls, it may be easy to adapt your house to passive solar heating or natural cooling. Of course, there are many possibilities for using these techniques even without ideal conditions. Many houses don't fit these conditions, so don't be discouraged if yours doesn't. For example, you can add an attached greenhouse for home heating to the east or west side of your house as long as the greenhouse receives adequate direct sunlight.

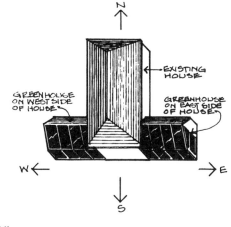

RECOMMENDATION

If your house is relatively long and thin with good southern exposure, it offers excellent potential for passive solar heating and natural cooling.

(6-11)

(15-20)

If the south walls are small and have little exposure to sunlight, consider active space heating and water heating or look for modest ways to use passive heating and cooling techniques.

(13,14)

For cooling, rooms facing south are easy to shade with overhangs, but those facing east and west have a tendency to overheat when the sun is low in the sky. Vertical shading devices like fences, awnings, and dense plants are needed to shade these walls and windows effectively.

(15)

(15-17)

B. FLOOR PLAN OF YOUR HOUSE

Interior spaces on the south side of the house can meet much of their heating and lighting requirements with the sun's energy. For the most effective use of passive techniques, it helps if rooms which are used during the day are located along the south wall. However, in many cases people have been able to bring sunlight and heat directly into north rooms.

An addition to your house can also serve as an opportunity for passive heat gain. You should look at your lot to see if there might be a sunny spot next to your house for a solar addition.

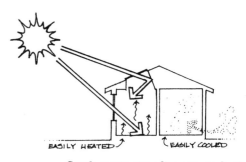

South rooms are often easy to heat.

RECOMMENDATION

Consider the rooms on the south side of your house. If they are day use rooms like the kitchen, family room, or home office, and they have good exposure to the sun, it's likely that passive space heating and cooling techniques will work effectively for you. If these same spaces are mostly on the north side of your house they will probably be easy to cool, but more difficult to heat passively. You should begin to more seriously consider active systems for water heating and space heating.

(6-11)
(15-20)

(13, 14)

C. SOUTH WALLS AND WINDOWS

Solar heat entering south facing windows will often more than offset the heat lost through the windows. You can construct a simple direct gain system by adding some method of storing the heat in the room and a way to insulate the windows at night to prevent heat loss. There are many other ways to use your south wall for passive systems. If you have space outside you can add an attached greenhouse. If space is limited in the south yard and views out to the south are not important, you can build a thermal storage wall which provides heat in the winter and natural cooling in the summer. Window box collectors can provide additional solar heat during daytime hours at low cost; check your sun chart to make sure the window in question has good winter sun exposure. Remember, your south wall should be within 30° of true south for these south wall techniques to function best.

(12)

(8)

(9)

(10)

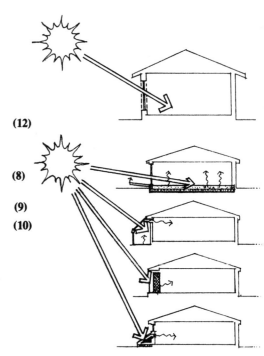

There are many techniques for using solar energy on south walls and windows.

RECOMMENDATION

Your house's south facing walls offer you the most direct and easily gained access to the sun by a variety of remodeling measures. The simplest heating technique is often to add more windows to this wall.

(6)

D. THE ROOF

The roof is often the sunniest place on your site and may have the fewest obstructions. It can be used for space heating, water heating, and natural cooling.

Your roof can be used for passive gain by adding skylights or clerestories. Although clerestories can be added to many kinds of roofs, flat roofs are especially suitable for clerestories. Skylights work best on sloped, south facing roofs. Certain precautions are necessary when adding skylights to your south facing roof. Because the winter sun angle is low in the sky, a skylight in a low pitched roof provides very little useful heat gain and, without night insulation, will increase heat loss. In the summer when the sun is higher, an unshaded skylight in a low pitched roof will greatly increase heat gain and the possibility of overheating your home. Hinged reflectors above the skylight can increase winter gain and shade the skylight from the direct sun in the summer, making it possible to use skylights effectively on gently sloping or flat roofs. A well placed, operable skylight can contribute to summer cooling by allowing rising warm air to escape.

(7)
(7)

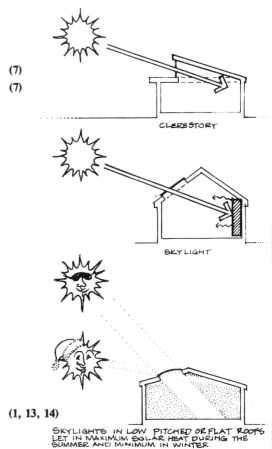

CLERESTORY

SKYLIGHT

SKYLIGHTS IN LOW PITCHED OR FLAT ROOFS LET IN MAXIMUM SOLAR HEAT DURING THE SUMMER AND MINIMUM IN WINTER.

Your roof can also serve as the location for collector panels for an active system. Look for an unshaded area free of vents, wires, and chimneys. Effective *collector angles* range from 30° to 60° and low pitched roofs may require the use of mounting brackets for proper tilt.

If your roof is flat, you probably have a good location for solar collectors. On a flat roof, collector angle can be easily adjusted with brackets.

(1, 13, 14)

On any kind of roof, the structure must be capable of supporting the additional weight of the collectors. Most newer roofs will have no difficulty supporting collectors.

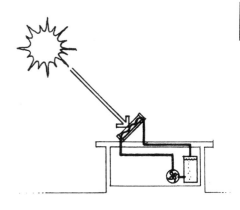

Another factor to take into account is the roofing material. It may be difficult to attach anything to roofing materials such as concrete or clay tile. Wood shingle or shake roofs are better, and metal and composition roofs allow for the easiest attachment of solar collectors.

If the roof is not suitable, collectors can also be mounted on the ground in a sunny place. Ground mounted collectors are often easier to build and maintain than those on a roof, and may be more easily integrated with your house's surroundings.

RECOMMENDATION

Determine the pitch and orientation of the south facing portion of your roof. Direct gain can be achieved with skylights on a roof pitched 45° or more, and with

(7)

clerestories, especially on flat roofs. With reflectors, (7)
skylights can be effective on roofs of less than 45° slope.
Active collectors can be mounted on any roof pitch with
brackets to orient them correctly. Almost any kind of (1, 13, 14)
openings in your roof will assist with summer cooling
through increased ventilation. (19)

Low cost homemade reflectors increase winter heat gain through horizontal skylights at the New Mexico Solar Energy Association offices. In summer, their angle is adjusted to provide shading.

E. STRUCTURAL CHARACTERISTICS

Your house is probably one of three kinds of construction.
• Wood Frame
• Post and Beam
• Masonry

Each type of construction has certain limitations and
certain opportunities.

Wood Frame

Wood frame construction uses walls built of 2x4s or 2x6s and covered with plywood, boards, or veneer. The principal advantage of wood frame construction is its flexibility and the ease with which it accepts remodeling.

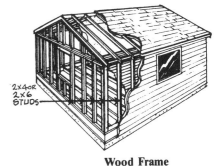

Wood Frame

In this type of construction, some walls bear the loads of the upper floors and roof and some merely serve as partitions. Even the load-bearing walls can have openings made in them if care is exercised in design and construction. If there is a particularly good opportunity to open a south-facing frame wall for direct gain through additional windows or by the addition of an attached solar greenhouse, don't let the load-bearing function of the wall deter you; just be careful about the design of the openings. **(6)** **(8)**

The main disadvantage of wood frame houses is that, unless constructed on a slab floor, they offer little in the way of heat storage mass for passive improvements.

Post and Beam

Some houses have the upper floor and roof loads carried through beams to posts or columns and then to the foundation. The panels located between posts in the walls are not load bearing and can be easily changed. Wood panels, for example, often can be replaced with glazing for direct gain or removed for access to a solar greenhouse. It is important, however, not to eliminate posts or their lateral supports. This type of construction tends to be lightweight and you will need to add heat storage materials to retain the solar heat you introduce. **(6, 8)**

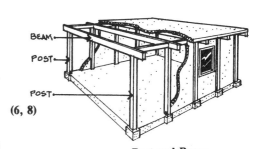

Post and Beam

Masonry

Houses made of solid masonry—concrete block, adobe, or brick used as the basic construction material, not just as veneer—have strong opportunities and strong limitations. With insulation added to the outside of the masonry, you have an excellent storage system to couple with direct gain from the sun's heat. The thermal mass of the house itself will absorb great amounts of the solar radiation and keep temperatures relatively stable. You can also add glazing to the outside of a south-facing masonry wall to create a thermal storage wall. **(6)** **(9)**

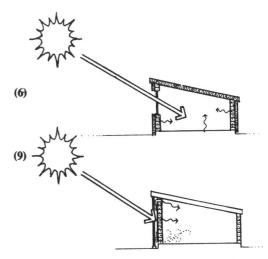

Passive Heating in Masonry Houses

The major limitation is that masonry walls are highly inflexible and difficult to penetrate with additional openings for direct gain. Consult an architect or engineer before you consider major alterations to a masonry wall.

RECOMMENDATION

Both wood frame and post and beam houses are easy to remodel for passive heating but will generally require the addition of mass for storage.

Masonry houses offer good opportunities for passive heating because of their built-in storage capacity. Be sure to get good advice about making openings through the masonry for additional solar gain.

F. HEAT STORAGE POSSIBILITIES

Heat entering your house directly or through collectors should be stored. Heat storage serves two functions in passive systems. One is to absorb excess heat to prevent overheating. The second is to provide usable reserve heat for sunless periods.

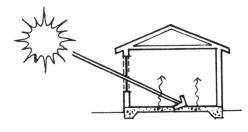

Storage is achieved with thermal mass, usually in the form of water, masonry, or rocks. This mass will absorb the excess heat which is collected during the day and release it when needed. If your solar house doesn't have enough thermal mass, excess solar energy may cause overheating.

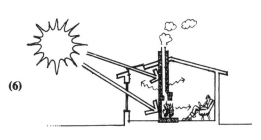

In passive approaches, thermal mass should ideally be in a position where the sun can strike it directly. For instance, if you have a slab floor and can add windows in the south wall in such a manner that sunlight will strike the floor, you have the potential for a passive system. **(6)**

If you are thinking of adding onto your existing house— either a solar greenhouse or another room facing to the south—you might consider a slab floor and a masonry or *water wall*. If you are not planning to add onto your house, you should think about adding masonry where the sun will strike it directly during the heating season. **(8)**

(6)

In an active system, the heat absorbed by the fluids (water or air) passing through the collectors must be stored for use. Water collectors generally use a well-insulated large fiberglass, steel, or concrete reservoir to store this heat; air collectors use a large container of rocks. You will need to find a place for these containers if you use an active system.

For an air collector designed to heat an insulated, 1500 square-foot house, you will need a storage space equal to the size of two typical American station wagons. This space would be filled with rocks to create a *rock storage system*. If your storage medium were water, you could do as well with about half this space.

The addition of mass to your house can improve its cooling capacity, too. During the day as air temperatures rise, any mass inside the house will absorb some of the heat, which makes the air cooler. As the air temperatures cool off at night the mass will give off some of its stored heat to the cooler air and be ready the next morning to absorb more daytime heat.

Cooling with Thermal Mass

RECOMMENDATION

If your house gets enough winter sun for you to consider solar space heating—either active or passive—you next need to look for ways to store the heat you collect. Although not all solar designs require heat storage, most do. This can often be a remodeling problem since storage usually requires space in or next to your house.

G. EXISTING MECHANICAL SYSTEMS

Your present heating or cooling system may influence your choice of solar options.

Your house will probably have one of the following types of heating:

- central systems include forced air or gravity systems with a furnace or heat pump, or circulating hot water or steam with a boiler;
- electric or gas unit heaters usually have controls in each room and include electric baseboard heaters or wall units;
- fireplaces or wood stoves.

Central systems tend to be readily adaptable to active solar space heating systems. Solar heat can be distributed through the same ducts or pipes that carry heat from the furnace or heat pump.

(13, 14)

For passive solar improvements, you may need to make some adjustments to your central system. With properly located return air inlets (the ones that bring air back to the furnace), a central air system can be used to circulate solar heated air to the rest of your house.

Your house may instead have individual heat sources in each room. These can be electric baseboard heaters, fan-forced electric or gas heaters in the wall or floor, or radiant heat in the ceiling. These systems can't be coupled directly with solar heating systems. They can, however, serve as *auxiliary systems,* and they have the advantage of allowing you to control each room individually.

RECOMMENDATION

A central heating system can often be adapted to circulate heat from either active or passive solar systems.

If you have unit heat sources in individual rooms, these will fit well with a passive system. An active system may require that you supplement or replace your unit heaters with a new central distribution system. **(6-11)**

H. OTHER REMODELING POSSIBILITIES

People often first think about using solar energy because they are considering some other addition. A common example is the solar greenhouse. Homeowners first think about adding a greenhouse and then realize that by attaching it properly to their house they can enhance their living space and provide heat at the same time.

If you are thinking of improving the natural light in your house, for example, consider putting some windows on the south side. If you are thinking of adding a room, consider a roof design that includes clerestories or can accommodate a collector.

This process can also be reversed. If you are thinking about adding a solar improvement to your house, you might consider what other changes you have been wanting to make. Chances are good that you can combine the two.

If you want to place collectors on the ground, think about arranging them to enclose a useful patio space or to form a windscreen. In redesigning the interior of your house or adding new space, be sure to look for opportunities to add thermal storage.

RECOMMENDATION

Whenever possible, try to accomplish several goals with each change to your house. This is almost always possible and will make your solar addition useful in many ways.

INTRODUCTION TO CHECK LISTS

Now you have looked at your house and site and should have some ideas about solar remodeling possibilities. Use these check lists to quickly review your work and proceed to Chapter 5 for more detailed information on options for your house.

CHECK LIST FOR WATER HEATING

A quick review will help you focus on solar water heating for your house. The first item is fairly critical. If you can't (1,2,3) answer yes to it, then solar water heating probably isn't feasible although you might still contact a designer to get another examination of your site. If you answer positively to the remaining items, then solar water heating will be easy to adapt to your house. To the extent you answer negatively, you will need assistance in working out the details of your system.

Critical Items

	Yes	No
1. Do you have an adequate roof or outdoor space next to the house oriented within 30° of south that receives sunlight throughout the year?	☐	☐

Useful Items

	Yes	No
2. Can your water heater tank be located in a heated room? Can the water pipes and the tank be insulated?	☐	☐
3. Could you place your water heater near the places you use major amounts of hot water?	☐	☐
4. Can your roofing surface easily accept new supports for collectors and new *flashings*?	☐	☐
5. Would collector panels on the roof of your house look acceptable?	☐	☐
6. Are you considering adding additional space which might provide a roof suitable for new collectors?	☐	☐

CHECKLIST FOR PASSIVE SPACE HEATING

Passive solar space heating tends to be the simplest and (6-11) most cost-effective way to use solar energy. However, it requires integrating many elements of your house and needs careful design.

Critical Items

	Yes	No
1. Do you have adequate unshaded south walls, roof, or outdoor space to use for a collection area?	☐	☐
2. Can your house be well insulated and weatherstripped?	☐	☐

Useful Items

	Yes	No
3. Are your day use spaces mainly along this sunny south wall?	☐	☐
4. Can your existing heating system be adjusted to provide less heat to those rooms that are solar heated while still providing necessary heat to those that are not?	☐	☐

31

	Yes	No
5. Can you find places inside your home to store the sun's heat using concrete, masonry, containers of water, or other materials?	☐	☐
6. Will your house's structural characteristics allow for modifications in the roof or south wall to add glazing?	☐	☐
7. Will your floor and foundations support the additional weight of storage materials?	☐	☐
8. Could you incorporate effective skylights or clerestories in your roof?	☐	☐
9. Are you considering adding additional space which could be passively solar heated?	☐	☐

CHECKLIST FOR ACTIVE SPACE HEATING

Active space heating is often a more expensive way of using the sun's heat. However, because of house orientation or shading of walls, this may be your best alternative. Carefully consider passive space heating before going on to this checklist.

(13, 14)

Critical Items

	Yes	No
1. Do you have adequate unshaded south roof or outdoor space to use for collector area?	☐	☐
2. Can your house be well insulated and weatherstripped?	☐	☐

Useful Items

	Yes	No
3. Do you have a central heating system? (This is most easily adapted to active space heating.)	☐	☐
4. Can you find a place for heat storage materials such as rock or water?	☐	☐
5. Can your roofing surface easily accept new supports for collectors and new flashing?	☐	☐
6. Would collector panels on the roof of your house look acceptable to you?	☐	☐
7. Are you considering adding additional space which could support collectors on the roof?	☐	☐

CHECKLIST FOR NATURAL COOLING

	Yes	No
1. Are there opportunities for cross ventilation?	☐	☐
2. Are there places to plant trees on the west or south?	☐	☐
3. Could you open up the house to shaded outdoor spaces?	☐	☐
4. Are there opportunities to make some tall spaces in the house which would allow vertical air movement?	☐	☐
5. Could you grow deciduous plants to shade sunny windows in the summer?	☐	☐
6. Could you screen windows to block summer sun?	☐	☐

Chapter 5 isn't meant to be read through from beginning to end. Unless you're simply curious about solar technologies, there's really no need to read the entire chapter. This chapter consists of a set of independent fact sheets which describe various options which may be appropriate for existing homes in our area. Some options are closely related to others, and these are clustered together. You may want to consider several related options in a cluster before you make your final decision.

Use Chapter 4 to decide which sections in this chapter will be helpful in making decisions about using solar energy in your home. Then read those fact sheets to learn more about how the options work, how much they cost, and where to go for more information. The cost figures on each sheet range from a low which is based on do-it-yourself costs using recycled materials to a high which is based on purchasing top quality materials and using contracted labor. Unusual circumstances may require more expensive remodeling. Similarly, each energy savings estimate is presented as a range to take into account differences in the quality of systems.

After reading about your recommended options, you should be able to make a well-informed decision about which solar improvement is best for you and your house. Once you reach that point, you can proceed directly to Chapter 6, which will help you with the design of your solar home improvement project.

1. FLAT PLATE ACTIVE

How it Works These water heaters consist of flat plate solar collectors, a storage tank, piping, pumps, and controls to assure proper functioning. Heat is collected by liquid flowing through solar collectors, usually mounted on a south-facing roof, and pumped to a storage tank for later use. The storage tank is similar in size to a conventional water heater.

Since water heating collectors are in use year-round, freezing is a potential problem. Freezing is usually prevented by either of two methods: (1) draining the collectors of water when freezing damage could occur, either manually or with automatic valves; (2) circulating a solution of antifreeze through the collectors to prevent freeze damage and transferring the heat collected to potable water via a heat exchanger.

Advantages/Disadvantages Because the collector area is not large, it is usually easy to find an unshaded space on the roof or in the yard suitable for the collector location. Because the collectors can be located separate from the storage tank, you have wide latitude in mounting the

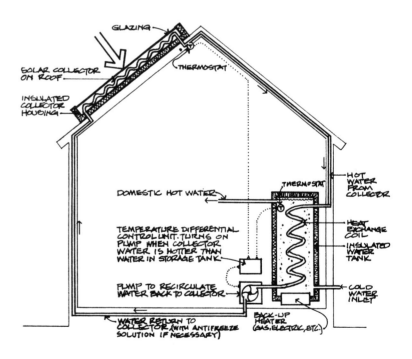

collectors. These systems are usually completely automatic and do not require active participation by occupants. Very limited annual maintenance may be required such as oiling pumps, cleaning strainers, testing antifreeze, or periodically flushing the system. A complete package

FLAT PLATE ACTIVE WATER HEATING

including all needed components can be purchased off-the-shelf from a large number of manufacturers and distributors. Because of the pumps and other controls, these systems cost more than other solar water heating systems. Flat plate active water heaters are the most common commercial solar water heaters.

House and Site Requirements

- Unshaded area on roof, wall, or yard for solar collectors (10 to 20 square feet per person in the house) facing within 30° of due south
- Location for storage tank, which may replace existing water heater
- Heat Storage: The storage tank should have a capacity of about 1.0 to 1.5 gallons per square foot of collector

Cost

Do-it-yourself	$12 to $30/square foot of collection area
Contractor Installed	$50 to $100/square foot of collection area, or a total of $2,000 to $5,000 for an average family

Energy Savings

Can provide 50% to 90% of water heating

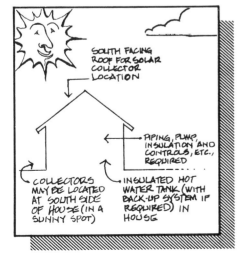

Resources

- *Solar Hot Water and Your Home.* National Solar Heating and Cooling Information Center, Washington, D.C.: U.S. Government Printing Office, 1978.

- *Hot Water from the Sun: A Consumer Guide to Solar Water Heating.* HUD, Washington, D.C.: U.S. Government Printing Office.

- *Installation Guidelines for Solar DHW Systems in One and Two Family Dwellings.* HUD, Washington, DC. Reprinted and distributed by Western SUN, P.O. Box 2770 Santa Fe, NM 87501.

35

2. FLAT PLATE THERMOSIPHON

How it Works *Thermosiphon* water heaters, also called natural convection water heaters or passive water heaters, consist of flat plate solar collectors, a storage tank, and piping. Heat is collected by liquid flowing through the solar collectors and the warmed fluid circulates by natural convection up to a storage tank located above the collectors. Thermosiphon collectors don't require auxillary power.

Since water heating is a year-round use, freezing is a potential problem. Freezing can be prevented by either of two methods: (1) draining the collectors of water when freezing damage could occur, either manually or with automatic valves and controls; (2) using a solution of antifreeze in the collectors to prevent freeze damage and transfer the heat collected to potable water with a heat exchanger.

Advantages/Disadvantages Because only a small area is needed for collectors, it is usually easy to find a sunny location on the roof or adjacent to the house. Since the collectors can be separate from the storage, this provides

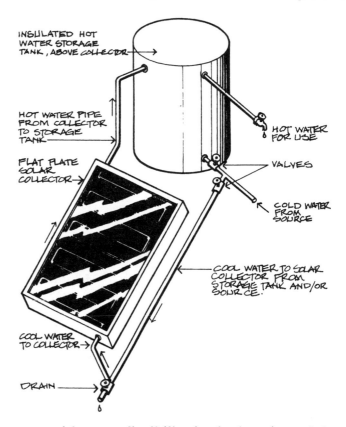

you with some flexibility in the location of these components. However, the storage tank must be located above the top of the solar collectors. On existing houses,

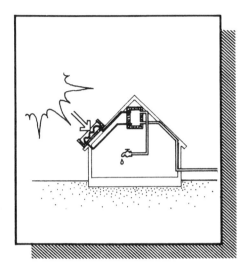

FLAT PLATE THERMOSIPHON WATER HEATING

this may be difficult to accomplish. No pumps are required for operation, making these water heaters easy to maintain. Since fewer components are required, thermosiphon systems cost less than most flat plate active water heaters.

House and Site Requirements

- Unshaded area on roof, or wall for solar collectors (10 to 20 square feet per person in the house) facing within 30° of due south
- Heated (preferred) location for storage tank above solar collectors and in close proximity
- When roof mounting tank, additional structural support is generally required

Cost

Do-it-yourself	$10 to $25/square foot of collection area
Contractor Installed	$30 to $60/square foot of collection area

Energy Savings

Can provide 50% to 90% of water heating

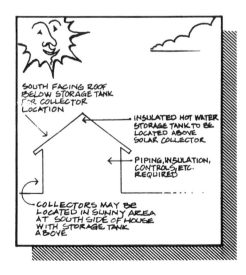

Resources

- *Hot Water from the Sun, A Consumer Guide to Solar Water Heating.* HUD, Washington, D.C.: U.S. Government Printing Office.
- *The Solar Water Heater Workshop Manual.* Ken Eklund et al, Seattle, Washington: Ecotope Group, 2nd ed., 1979.
- *The Solar Water Heater Book.* Bryenton, et al, Toronto, Canada: Renewable Energy in Canada, 1980.

3. BATCH

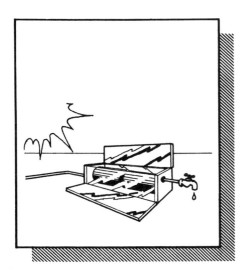

How it Works These water heaters, also called breadbo or passive water heaters, incorporate the storage tank as part of the collector. A storage tank is enclosed in an insulated box with south glazing or may be placed in a solar greenhouse. The water tank is blackened so that it will absorb sunshine and heat the water inside. The tank can be made from a variety of materials, the most common choice is the inside tank of a conventional water heater. The cold water pipe to your existing water heater i interrupted so that the water is first routed through the batch heater to preheat it. Freezing in cold weather is not usually a problem due to the large volume of warm water in the tank. However, the pipes to and from the batch heater must be protected from freezing.

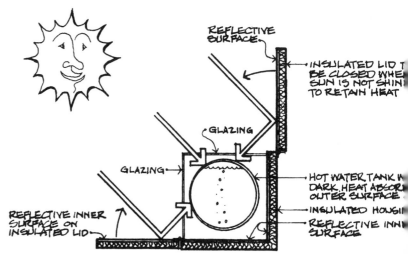

SECTION THROUGH "BREADBOX" WATER HEATER

Advantages/Disadvantages Freezing of connecting pipes can be a problem. The main disadvantage of a batch heater is heat loss at night or during cloudy weather. For this reason, the box should be provided with an insulating cover to reduce losses. The movable insulation cover is often covered with a reflector to bounce additional sunlight onto the water tank when the cover is open. Manually operated insulating covers require more persona

SOUTH ELEVATION OF "BREADBOX" WATER HEATER

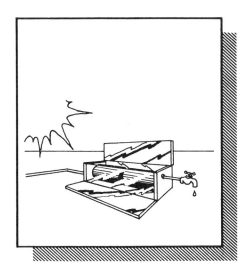

BATCH WATER HEATING

effort for proper operation. These batch heaters are simpler and less expensive than water heating systems which have separate collectors and storage.

The New Mexico Solar Energy Association has developed several efficient batch water heater designs that do not require daily attention. For more information, stop by their Santa Fe office to see demonstration models or send for the May 1981 issue of their *Sunpaper* ($2 post paid) which contains a summary of their batch water heater research and development.

House and Site Requirements

- Unshaded area facing within 30° of due south
- Collection area in proximity to existing water heater
- Several smaller tanks are often used rather than one large tank, to get the required collection area and collector/storage ratio

Cost

Do-it-yourself	$100 to $400
Contractor Installed	$600 to $1,000

Energy Savings

Can provide 30% to 70% of water heating

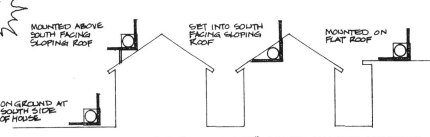

POSSIBLE LOCATIONS FOR "BREADBOX" SOLAR WATER HEATER

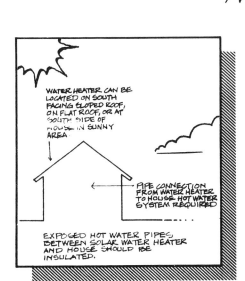

WATER HEATER CAN BE LOCATED ON SOUTH FACING SLOPED ROOF, ON FLAT ROOF, OR AT SOUTH SIDE OF HOUSE IN SUNNY AREA.

PIPE CONNECTION FROM WATER HEATER TO HOUSE HOT WATER SYSTEM REQUIRED.

EXPOSED HOT WATER PIPES BETWEEN SOLAR WATER HEATER AND HOUSE SHOULD BE INSULATED.

Resources

- *Breadbox Water Heater Plans*. Steve Baer, Zomeworks Corp., Box 712, Albuquerque, NM 87103, 1975.
- *How to Build a Passive Solar Water Heater*. Horace McCracken, Boulevard, CA: Mountain Press, 1978.
- "Batch Water Heater Update" by Bristol Stickney, *Sunpaper: Bulletin of the New Mexico Solar Energy Association,* Vol. 6 No. 5, May 1981.

4. SWIMMING POOLS

How it Works Pools are particularly well suited to solar heating. The existing pool circulating system is usually used for pumping the pool water through the solar collectors. The pool itself serves as the storage medium, while the existing pump and heater provide circulation and backup. Solar pool heating is highly efficient since pools need be heated only moderately above air temperatures. Usually, the solar collectors are unglazed for summer only heating, while glazed solar panels are required for year-round pools. Floating pool covers are often used to reduce heat loss.

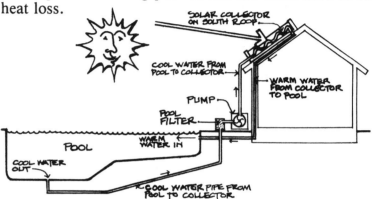

SECTION - SWIMMING POOL HEATING

Advantages/Disadvantages These systems generally require a sizable collector area to provide adequate pool heating. However, since the collectors can be located separate from the pool, you have considerable flexibility in choosing the best location to install them. Systems using unglazed solar collectors are usually relatively inexpensive and will pay for themselves in energy savings in a few years. Solar heaters will generally maintain comfortable swimming temperatures about twice as long as an unheated pool.

House and Site Requirements

- A large unshaded south roof or yard area facing within 30° of due south (60% of the pool area with unglazed collectors).
- Adequate space for piping from collector area to pool equipment

Cost

Do-it-yourself	$2 to $10/square foot of collector area
Contractor Installed	$7 to $20/square foot of collector area

Energy Savings

Can provide up to 100% of your pool heating needs in the spring, summer, and fall

Resources

- *How To Design and Build A Solar Swimming Pool Heater.* Copper Development Association, Inc., 405 Lexington Ave., NY, NY 10017.
- *Solar Heat For Swimming Pools.* Douglas E. Root, Jr., et al, Winter Park, FL: Florida Conservation Foundation.

5. HOT TUBS

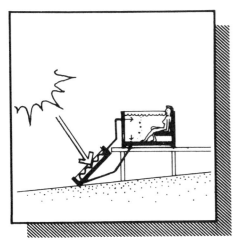

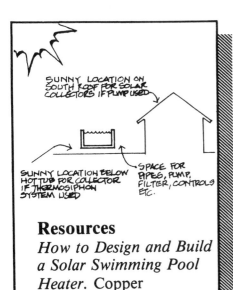

SECTION - HOT TUB WITH
THERMOSIPHON SYSTEM

Resources

How to Design and Build a Solar Swimming Pool Heater. Copper Development Association, Inc., 405 Lexington Ave., NY, NY 10017.

How it Works Hot tub or spa heating is similar to pool heating, except that spas are generally used on a year round basis at temperatures around 100ºF. In these applications, glazed solar collectors are used to collect the

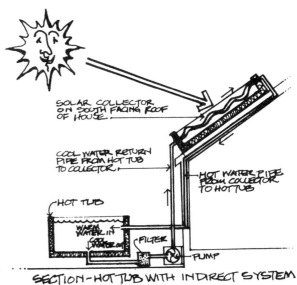

SECTION - HOT TUB WITH INDIRECT SYSTEM

sun's energy. The hot tub is used for the heat storage tank. The collectors are usually mounted above the tub and drain back into the spa whenever the pump is turned off. Solar energy is often used as a back-up energy source for hot tub heating.

Advantages/Disadvantages The collection area required for a typical hot tub is small, only 50 to 100 square feet. The collectors may be located in a suitable sunny location on a roof or in the yard. The cost for solar heating equipment for a spa is more expensive than pool collectors, since the collectors are usually glazed.

House and Site Requirements

- An unshaded south roof or yard area for solar collection (3-5 panels) facing within 30º of due south
- Adequate space for piping from solar collectors to spa

Cost

Do-it-yourself	$5 to $20/square foot of collection area
Contractor Installed	$40 to $70/square foot of collection area

Energy Savings

Can provide a substantial portion of your hot tub heating needs

6. DIRECT GAIN SOUTH WALL AND WINDOWS

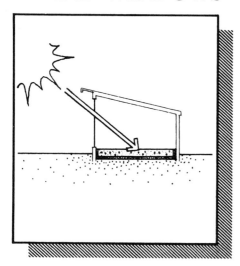

How it Works Direct gain is the simplest way to use solar energy in the home. Sunlight is admitted directly into living spaces through south-facing windows for daytime heating. You can use direct gain heating by adding south windows or glass doors to your house. Well-positioned south windows can provide heat on winter days, and they can be shaded in summer by overhangs or deciduous vegetation to prevent overheating. If your house has masonry floors or walls, solar heat will be stored in these materials, providing heating through the night.

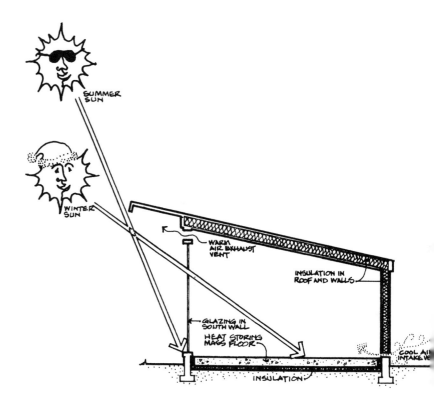

Advantages/Disadvantages South windows are inexpensive and easy to add in most houses. The same windows can provide views, lighting, and ventilation as well as solar heating. Construction is easy in wood frame houses, but more difficult in those with masonry walls. South windows will provide mostly daytime heating unless heat storage materials are incorporated. Additional windows also cause increased heat loss unless conservation measures such as adding movable insulation are taken. Overheating may occur in the summer unless shading is provided.

Break time in a direct gain remodeling job.

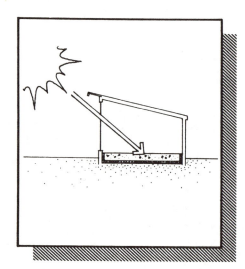

DIRECT GAIN SOUTH WALL AND WINDOWS SPACE HEATING

House and Site Requirements

- South wall facing within 30° of due south, unshaded in heating season
- Living spaces needing daytime heating located along the south wall
- Space for additional south windows
- Opportunities to add heat storage materials (preferred)

Cost

Do-it-yourself	$3 to $6/square foot of collection area
Contractor Installed	$5/square foot of collection area and up

Energy Savings

Each square foot of glass heats from three to nine square feet of floor space, with adequate heat storage and insulation

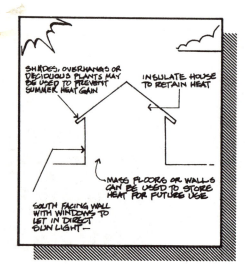

Resources

The Passive Solar Energy Book. Edward Mazria, Emmaus, PA: Rodale Press, 1979.

7. DIRECT GAIN SKYLIGHTS AND CLERESTORIES

How it Works Sunlight is admitted directly in the living space through south-facing skylights or high windows called clerestories. The sunlight is absorbed and turned to heat providing winter heating during the daytime. You can use direct gain by adding south skylights or clerestories in

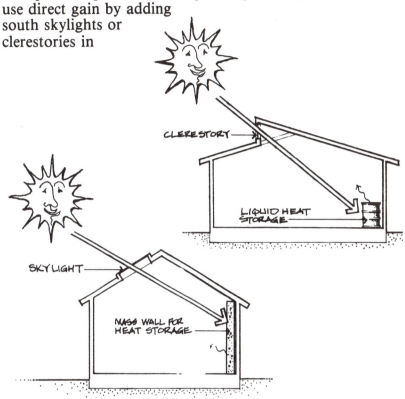

your roof. If your house has masonry floors or walls, solar heat will be stored in these materials, providing heating later in the evening. Skylights must be shaded or vented in summer to prevent overheating.

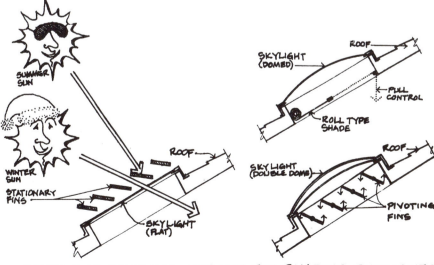

SECTIONS SHOWING METHODS FOR SHADING SKYLIGHTS

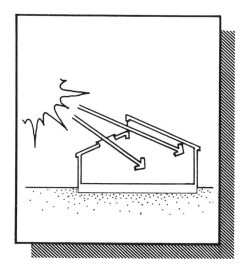

DIRECT GAIN SKYLIGHTS AND SPACE HEATING CLERESTORIES

Advantages/Disadvantages Skylights and clerestories are often more costly to add than south windows. However, they can often provide solar heat to rooms that are not located on the south wall and can also provide lighting and ventilation. Skylights need to be shaded in summertime to prevent overheating, and insulated or double-glazed to prevent excessive heat loss.

House and Site Requirements

- Unshaded roof area facing within 30° of due south
- Living spaces requiring daytime heating located below skylight or clerestory
- For skylights, a roof tilted at least 45° above horizontal to take advantage of winter sunshine, unless reflectors are used

Cost

Do-it-yourself	$5 to $8/square foot of collection area
Contractor Installed	$7 to $12/square foot of collection area, or more

Energy Savings

- Each square foot of glass heats from three to nine square feet of floor space, with adequate heat storage and insulation
- Can provide up to 30% of your winter heating (higher fractions are possible with heat storage)

Resources

- *The Passive Solar Energy Book.* Edward Mazria, Emmaus, PA: Rodale Press, 1979.
- *Low-Cost Energy Efficient Shelter.* Eugene Eccli, ed., Emmaus, PA: Rodale Press, 1976.

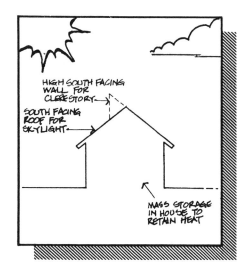

8. ATTACHED GREENHOUSE

How it Works A south-facing solar greenhouse, also called sunroom, solarium, or conservatory, can often be added to an existing house. Sunlight is admitted into the greenhouse where it is absorbed and turned to heat. Because a solar greenhouse is tightly sealed, heat builds up; by opening windows, doors, and other vents between the greenhouse and the house, warm air from the greenhouse will move by natural convection into the house, providing heating. To store excess solar energy and provide heating at night, thermal mass should be incorporated in the greenhouse. This heat storage can be of masonry materials such as concrete and brick or can be water stored in containers. Ventilation is essential to prevent overheating in the summer.

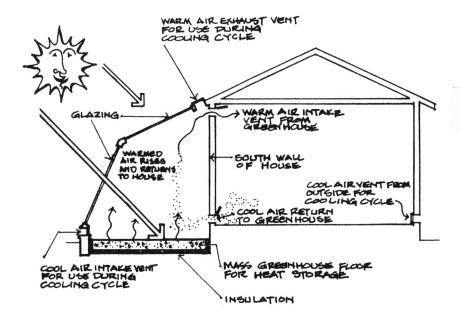

ATTACHED GREENHOUSE

Advantages/Disadvantages Greenhouses can be simple, relatively low cost projects for do-it-yourselfers. Greenhouses can also be elegant, beautifully designed additions to your home—the choice is yours. The design of the greenhouse depends on how you want to use it. A greenhouse can help heat your home, provide a place for growing plants, and add an attractive living space to your house. Heat storage can be added easily in the form of water in dark-colored containers. However, if adequate summer ventilation or shading is not incorporated, overheating can occur. Using movable insulation will help to reduce nighttime heat loss.

ATTACHED GREENHOUSE
SPACE HEATING

House and Site Requirements

- Unshaded south wall area facing within 30° of due south or places along the east or west side of the house where a south-facing sunroom could be added.
- Living spaces requiring heating located along south (preferred)
- Adjacent yard space to accomodate greenhouse

Cost

Do-it-yourself	$5 to $12/square foot of floor area
Contractor Installed	$30 to $75/square foot of floor area

Energy Savings

Heats itself plus an area of the adjacent house up to twice its size.

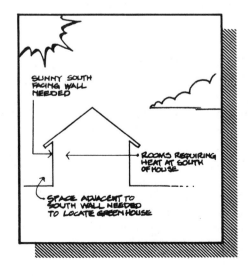

Resources

- *The Food and Heat Producing Solar Greenhouse.* Bill Yanda and Rick Fisher, Santa Fe, New Mexico: John Muir Publications, 2nd ed., 1980.
- *The Solar Greenhouse Book.* James C. McCullagh, Emmaus, PA: Rodale Press, 1978.
- *Building Your Solar Greenhouse: A Do It Yourself Construction Guide,* Erik Aaboe, Amy Matthei and Lucinda Marshall, New Mexico Solar Energy Association, Santa Fe, NM 1980.

9. THERMAL STORAGE WALL

How it Works In this approach, also called *Trombe wall* or *water wall*, masonry or water is placed directly behind south-facing glazing. Sunlight enters through the glazing, strikes the dark-colored heat storage materials and

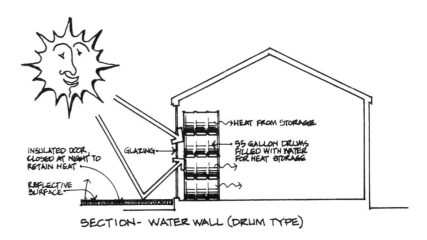

SECTION- WATER WALL (DRUM TYPE)

is absorbed and turned to heat. The heat is conducted through the wall and into the house. In addition, during the day, warmed air between the glazing and wall surface can circulate naturally to the interior space by means of vents. If your home already has masonry walls, you may be able to convert portions of your south walls to thermal storage walls quite inexpensively by adding *double glazing*.

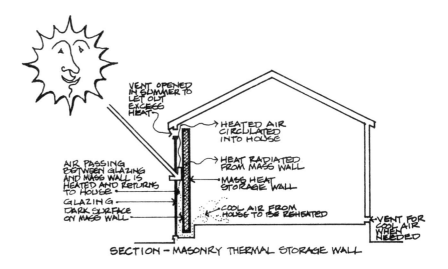

SECTION - MASONRY THERMAL STORAGE WALL

Advantages/Disadvantages Thermal storage walls have several advantages. They tend to moderate temperature swings in the house, since they heat up steadily and cool off slowly. Also, masonry walls delay peak heating until nighttime, when it is most needed. Since

THERMAL STORAGE WALL
SPACE HEATING

the heat storage is concentrated in the south wall, the remainder of the house can be constructed of light wood frame. Unless your home already has masonry walls, thermal storage walls are a major structural addition. Adding a masonry or water wall to a house will usually require special foundation design and will be relatively costly.

House and Site Requirements

* Unshaded south wall area facing within 30° of due south
* Living spaces requiring heating located along south side of house
* An existing solid masonry wall on the south (preferred)

Cost

Do-it-yourself	$8 to $12/square foot of collection area ($3 to $7 over existing masonry)
Contractor Installed	$10 to $40/square foot of collection area ($5 to $20 over existing masonry)

Energy Savings

Each square foot of storage wall heats from one to four square feet of living area

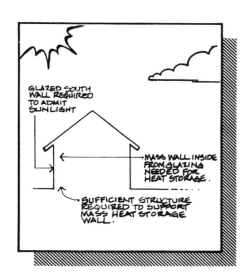

Resources

* *Thermal Storage Wall Manual.* New Mexico Solar Energy Association, P.O. Box 2004, Santa Fe, NM 87501.
* *Passive Solar Energy Book.* Edward Mazria, Emmaus, PA: Rodale Press, 1979.

10. WINDOW BOX COLLECTOR

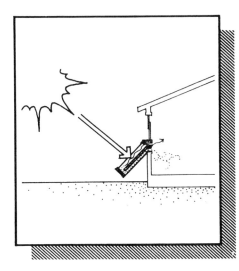

How it Works These simple air heating collectors operate by natural convection, collecting hot air in a separate solar collector and circulating this air to the house. They are ideal small retrofits, as they require little or no modification of the building and can be removed for the summer. These collectors are particularly suitable for providing 20% to 30% of the heating requirements of a room, and are used to supply daytime heating needs. They are best suited to houses with south-facing double-hung windows.

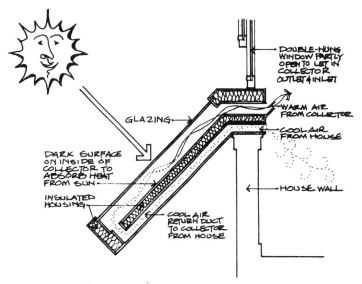

DOUBLE-HUNG WINDOW PARTLY OPEN TO LET IN COLLECTOR OUTLET & INLET

WARM AIR FROM COLLECTOR

COOL AIR FROM HOUSE

GLAZING

DARK SURFACE ON INSIDE OF COLLECTOR TO ABSORB HEAT FROM SUN

HOUSE WALL

INSULATED HOUSING

COOL AIR RETURN DUCT TO COLLECTOR FROM HOUSE

SECTION - WINDOW BOX SOLAR COLLECTOR

Advantages/Disadvantages When properly designed, these small air collectors can provide heat from the sun as efficiently as an active solar heating system, without any fans or controls. When window box collectors are properly designed, cold air stagnates in the collector box at night, preventing reverse convection without the use of dampers. Also, since window box collectors are removable in summer, overheating is not a problem. Their chief disadvantage is that they can only heat a small area.

WINDOW BOX COLLECTOR SPACE HEATING

House and Site Requirements

- Unshaded south wall or area south of house
- Living spaces requiring heating located along the south
- Double-hung windows on south side of house (preferred)

Cost

Do-it-yourself	$3 to $6/square foot of collection area
Contractor Installed	$6 to $15/square foot of collection area

Energy Savings

Can provide up to 30% of the winter heating needs of the room to which they're attached

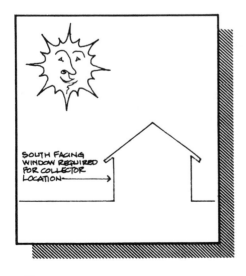

SOUTH FACING WINDOW REQUIRED FOR COLLECTOR LOCATION

Resources

- "Retrofitting with Natural Convection Collectors" by Scott Morris, *Sunpaper: Bulletin of the New Mexico Solar Energy Association,* Vol. 5, No. 5., May, 1980.
- *Window Mounted Solar Collector,* Scott Morris, New Mexico Solar Energy Association, P.O. Box 2004, Santa Fe, NM 87501.

11. VERTICAL AIR COLLECTOR

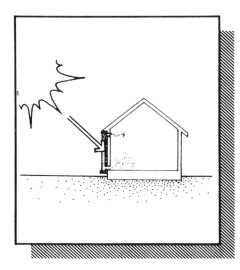

How it Works These simple air heating collectors, also called natural convection air collectors, thermosiphon air panels, or wall collectors, operate by circulating air from the house through a flat plate collector and back into the building by natural convection. They are usually mounted on a south-facing wall of a house. These collectors provide 20% to 30% of the heating requirements of the house, making them particularly suitable for supplying daytime heating needs. The use of heat storage can help provide greater savings, but may be difficult for existing houses.

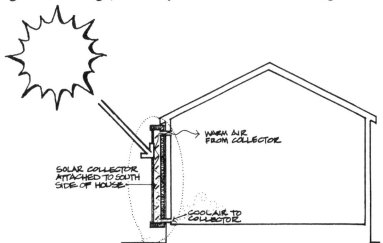

VERTICAL COLLECTOR ON HOUSE

Advantages/Disadvantages When properly designed, vertical air collectors will provide heat from the sun as efficiently as an active solar heating system, even though no fans or controls are used. They also have an advantage over other passive solar designs in that the collector can be thermally isolated from the heated space, and so does not become a source of heat loss at night. These collectors should be shaded and vents closed off tightly to prevent summer overheating. Their chief disadvantage is that they provide daytime heating only.

House and Site Requirements
- Unshaded south wall facing within 30° of due south
- Living spaces requiring heating located along the south wall

Cost

Do-it-yourself	$3 to $7/square foot of collection area
Contractor Installed	$6 to $15/square foot of collection area

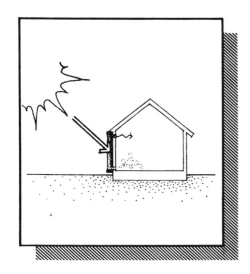

VERTICAL AIR CIRCULATION

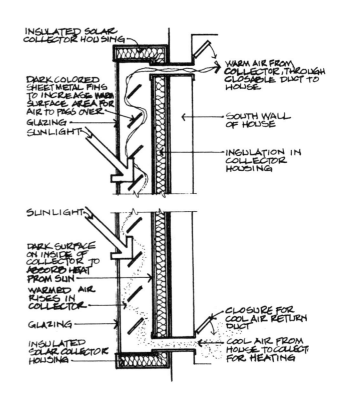

INSULATED SOLAR COLLECTOR HOUSING

DARK COLORED SHEET METAL FINS TO INCREASE WARM SURFACE AREA FOR AIR TO PASS OVER

GLAZING

SUNLIGHT

WARM AIR FROM COLLECTOR, THROUGH CLOSABLE DUCT TO HOUSE

SOUTH WALL OF HOUSE

INSULATION IN COLLECTOR HOUSING

SUNLIGHT

DARK SURFACE ON INSIDE OF COLLECTOR TO ABSORB HEAT FROM SUN

WARMED AIR RISES IN COLLECTOR

GLAZING

INSULATED SOLAR COLLECTOR HOUSING

CLOSURE FOR COOL AIR RETURN DUCT

COOL AIR FROM HOUSE TO COLLECTOR FOR HEATING

Energy Savings

- Each square foot of collector heats from one to three square feet of living area
- Can provide some nighttime heating with the addition of heat storage

Resources

- "Retrofitting with Natural Convection Collectors" by Scott Morris, *Sun Paper,* Bulletin of the New Mexico Solar Energy Association, Vol. 5, No. 5, May, 1980.
- "Design Concepts for Convective Air Collectors" by Scott Morris, *Sunpaper: Bulletin of the New Mexico Solar Energy Association,* Vol. 2, No. 9, September, 1977

SUNNY LOCATION ON SOUTH WALL REQUIRED FOR MOUNTING VERTICAL SOLAR COLLECTOR.

12. MOVABLE INSULATION

How it Works Movable insulation is also called window shutters, night shutters, or window insulation. In a well-insulated building, glazed openings (windows, glass doors, skylights) are usually the single largest source of heat loss. Passive solar heating relies on large south-facing glazing and is particularly susceptible to heat loss through the glazing. Movable insulation can be placed over glazed areas at night to reduce heat losses significantly. It can take many forms, including sliding panels, hinged shutters, and roll-down curtains. All these methods have one essential thing in common—they rely on a tight fit to work well.

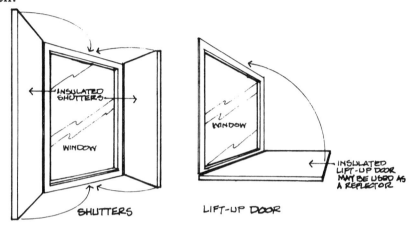

Advantages/Disadvantages The placement of the insulation may be by manual operation or it can be automatic. Manually operated devices depend on you for proper operation. Automatic devices do not require you to move shutters or drapes regularly, but are more complex and costly. However, they are especially useful in difficult-to-reach areas and for moving large insulating panels. Movable insulation also offers several secondary benefits. The same device can often be used for shading in summer, and when located outside the glass can be used as a reflector to bounce additional sunlight into the house when desired.

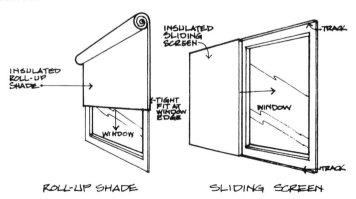

MOVABLE INSULATION

House and Site Requirements

Adequate storage space for movable insulation when in open position, either on top or at sides

Cost

| Do-it-yourself | $2 to $5 per square foot |
| Contractor Installed | $5 to $20 per square foot |

Energy Savings

- Can reduce your winter heating requirements by 20% to 30%

- Can also reduce summer cooling needs

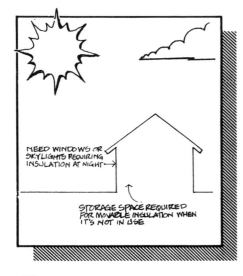

Resources

- *Movable Insulation: A Guide to Reducing Heating and Cooling Losses Through The Windows in Your House.* William K. Langdon, Emmaus, PA: Rodale Press, 1980.

- *Thermal Shades and Shutters: Over 100 Schemes for Reducing Heat Loss Through Windows.* William A. Shurcliff, Andover, MA: Brick House Publishing Co., 1980.

13. AIR COLLECTORS WITH ROCK STORAGE

How it Works Solar energy is collected by active solar air heating panels and is pumped to a large storage bin of rocks. Fans, dampers, ductwork, and controls are required for proper operation. Collectors are usually mounted on a south-facing roof but can also be located in your yard or against your south wall. The storage bin may be located in the basement, garage, utility building, underground, or house if space is available. Heat is provided to your home automatically and is usually controlled by a thermostat.

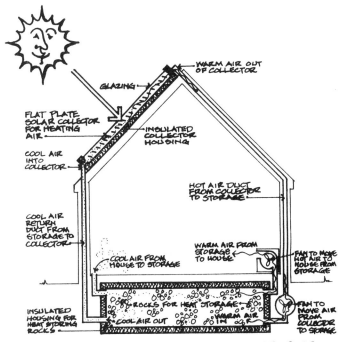

AIR COLLECTORS WITH ROCK STORAGE

Advantages/Disadvantages These systems generally require a sizable collector area to provide a significant portion of your space heating requirements. However, since the collectors can be located separate from the storage bin and the house, you have considerable flexibility in installing the solar equipment in the best location. Heat can be added to any spaces in your house, not just those on the south wall with good solar exposure. The rock storage usually occupies a large area, which may be difficult to find in an existing house. Also, the air ducts are large and may be difficult to add to a house. These systems are complex and should be carefully designed. If not properly engineered and installed, these systems may perform poorly.

AIR COLLECTORS WITH ROCK STORAGE

House and Site Requirements

- Unshaded south roof, wall, or yard area facing within 30° of due south (the collector area should be one-quarter to one-sixth of the floor space to be heated)
- Adequate space for rock storage
- Adequate space for ductwork, fan, and controls
- An existing forced air heating system for heat distribution (desirable)

Cost

Do-it-yourself	$10 to $35/square foot of collection area
Contractor Installed	$30 to $75/square foot of collection area

Energy Savings

Can heat an area two to six times the collector area

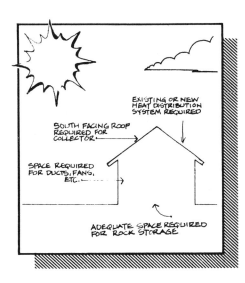

Resources

- *The Solar Home Book.* Bruce Anderson, Harrisville, NH: Cheshire Books, 1976.
- *Fundamentals of Solar Heating.* Prepared by the Sheet Metal and Air Conditioning Contractors National Association for USDOE. Springfield, VA: National Technical Information Service, (NTIS –HCP/N4038-01), January, 1978.
- *Model-TEA Solar Heating System Construction Manual.* Peter Temple and Jennifer Adams, Harrisville, NH: Total Environmental Action, 1980.

14. LIQUID COLLECTORS WITH WATER STORAGE

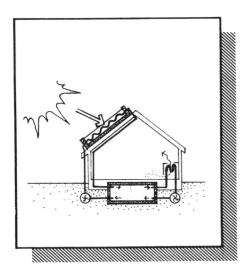

How it Works Solar energy is collected by active solar water heating panels and is usually stored in a large water storage tank. Pumps, valves, piping, and controls are required for proper operation. Collectors are usually mounted on a south-facing roof, but can also be placed in your yard or against a south-facing wall. The storage tank can be located in the garage, basement, utility building, underground, or house if space is available. Heat is provided to your home automatically, usually through a central heating system. Domestic water heating is also usually provided by the solar heating system.

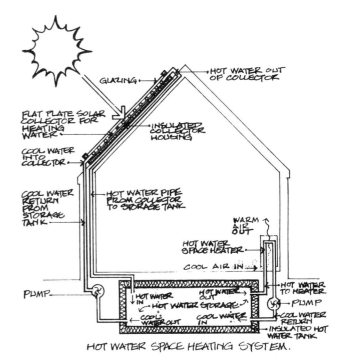

HOT WATER SPACE HEATING SYSTEM.

Advantages/Disadvantages These systems require a substantial solar collection area to provide a significant portion of your space heating needs. Since the collectors can be located separate from the storage tank and the house, you have considerable flexibility in locating the solar collectors to best receive winter sunshine. Heat can be added to any spaces in your house, not just those on the south wall with good solar exposure. Although the connecting pipes are usually small, there may be some difficulties in adding them to your home. The storage tank size is related to collector area but typically occupies the space of a small bathroom. These systems are complex and should be carefully designed. If not properly engineered and installed, these systems may perform poorly.

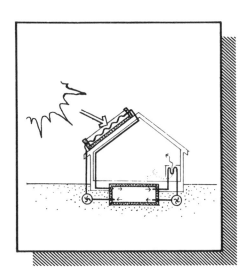

LIQUID COLLECTORS WITH WATER STOR

House and Site Requirements

- Unshaded south roof, wall, or yard area facing within 30° of due south (the collector area should be one-quarter to one-sixth of the floor space to be heated)
- Adequate space for water storage tank
- An existing forced air heating system or a radiant hot water floor or ceiling (desirable)

Cost

Do-it-yourself	$15 to $35/square foot of collection area
Contractor Installed	$40 to $100/square foot of collection area

Energy Savings

Can heat an area two to six times the collector area

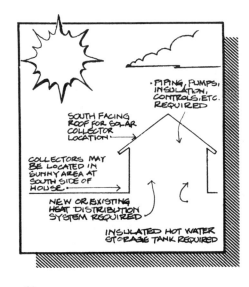

Resources:

The Solar Home Book. Bruce Anderson, Harrisville, NH: Cheshire Books, 1976.

15. WINDOW SHADING

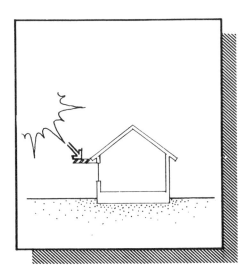

How it Works A major source of heat gain in houses is direct sunlight entering through unshaded windows. If sunlight can be excluded from the interior, the house will be cooler and use of air conditioning can be reduced or eliminated. Windows can be shaded by planting trees or

DECIDUOUS TREES FOR SUMMER SHADING

shrubs next to the house. Windows can also be shaded by adding devices on outside walls to cast shadows on the glass at appropriate times of the day. These devices could be awnings, canopies, louvers, "eyebrows," or other types. They need to be designed carefully for their specific locations. Windows on the south side need horizontal shades, while those on the west need vertical devices to protect from low sun angles.

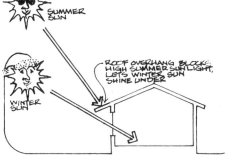

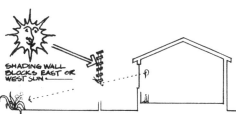

ROOF OVERHANG FOR SHADING   SHADING WITH WALL OR SCREEN

Advantages/Disadvantages No work needs to be done inside the house, minimizing disruption of activities. Most devices are low to moderate in cost. Structural support from outside walls needs to be adequate, and wind loads need to be considered in design. Fabric awnings may need replacement periodicially due to deterioration from sun and wind. Designs should not trap hot air at the top, nor interfere with free ventilation through windows.

WINDOW SHADING

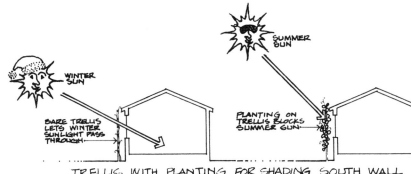

TRELLIS WITH PLANTING FOR SHADING SOUTH WALL

House and Site Requirements

- Adequate structure for support
- Access for construction and maintenance
- Adequate yard setback

Cost

Do-it-yourself	$10 to $100 per window
Contractor Installed	$20 to $200 per window

Energy Savings

Varies greatly; can reduce undesirable heat gain significantly

Resources

- *Design with Climate.* Victor Olgyay, Princeton, NJ: Princeton University Press, 1963.
- *Solar Control & Shading Devices.* Aladar and Victor Olgyay, Princeton, NJ: Princeton University Press, 1976.

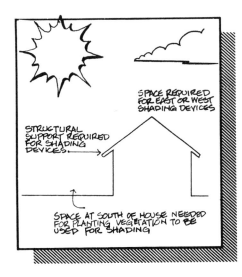

16. WINDOW SHADING MATERIALS

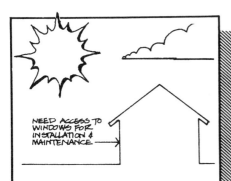

How it Works A major source of heat gain in houses is direct sunlight entering through unshaded windows. If sunlight can be excluded from the interiors, the house will be cooler and more comfortable and use of air conditioning can be reduced or eliminated. Special types of glass and materials applied to existing glass are two ways to reduce solar heat gain. Reflecting or mirror glass can reduce heat gain up to 75%; heat absorbing or tinted glass up to 40%. Reflecting films can be applied to the insides of existing windows, reducing heat gain up to 75%. Shade-type screens work like tiny louvers punched out of thin metal screening, or take the form of tiny round holes punched in dark plastic.

Advantages/Disadvantages Solar films can reduce heat gain substantially, without obstructing views. Window exteriors can take on mirror-like reflectance, increasing privacy. Some films reverse their effect at night, becoming mirror-like from inside but permitting views from outside. Application of tinted or heat-absorbing glass can increase heat gain of the glass itself, which can lead to breakage if the windows are improperly installed. Heat-absorbing and reflecting glass are expensive, must be cut to size before shipment, and can be difficult to replace quickly if broken. Shade screens replace normal insect screens and preserve views, but slightly decrease daylight and air circulation.

House and Site Requirements

Access to windows for installation/cleaning/replacement

Cost

Do-it-yourself	$1 to $3 per square foot
Contractor Installed	$2 to $6 per square foot

Energy Savings

Can reduce heat gain significantly

Resources

• *Solar Control and Shading Devices.* Aladar and Victor Olgyay, Princeton, NJ: Princeton University Press, 1976.
• *Hawaii Home Energy Book.* Jim Pearson, Honolulu, HI: The University Press of Hawaii and The Research Corporation of the University of Hawaii, 1978.

17. LANDSCAPE DESIGN

How it Works A major source of heat gain in houses is direct solar gain through unshaded windows. If solar radiation can be blocked from these surfaces the spaces will be cooler. Also, air flow through houses contributes greatly to evaporative cooling and natural comfort. Carefully selected trees and shrubs can provide shade, reducing radiant heat gain through windows and lowering the surface temperatures of walls and roofs. Shading can reduce the temperatures of paved areas adjacent to the house, decreasing the heat which can be carried into the house by breezes. Trees and shrubs can be located to direct breezes into windows, thus increasing air flow through the house.

Advantages/Disadvantages Landscaping upgrades the appearance and value of houses. Plants require periodic maintenance and upkeep. Privacy can be enhanced by landscaping but air circulation can be reduced if plantings are too thick or too close to the house. Views can be framed by trees but also can be blocked. Tall-growing plants can shade solar collectors and can encroach into neighboring yards.

House and Site Requirements
- Adequate space for planting and for size of mature plants
- Green (or greenish) thumb

Cost

Do-it-yourself	$0 and up
Contractor Installed	$20 and up

Energy Savings
Can reduce heat gain significantly

Resources
- *Landscape Design That Saves Energy.* Anne Moffat and Marc Schiler, New York: William Morrow & Co., 1981.
- *Plants/People/and Environmental Quality.* Gary O. Robinette, Washington, D.C.: U.S. Department of the Interior, 1972.
- *Landscape Planning for Energy Conservation.* American Society of Landscape Architects Foundation, Reston, VA: Environmental Design Press, 1977.

18. CROSS VENTILATION

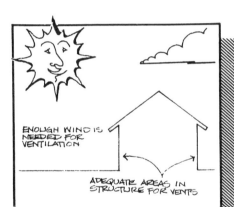

ENOUGH WIND IS NEEDED FOR VENTILATION

ADEQUATE AREAS IN STRUCTURE FOR VENTS

Resources

- *Design with Climate.*
Victor Olgyay,
Princeton, NJ: Princeton
University Press, 1963.
- *Hawaii Home Energy
Book.* Jim Pearson,
Honolulu, HI: The
University Press of Hawaii
and The Research
Corporation of the
University of Hawaii, 1978.

How it Works In a warm climate a gentle breeze evaporates moisture from the skin, keeping us cool in all but the most humid conditions. Correctly locating openings in outside walls permits breezes to flow through the house, providing a cooling effect. Warm air created by lights, cooking, people's bodies, and other sources can be flushed out of the house by cooler outside air. This action requires both inlets on the windward side and outlets on the leeward side; a single opening will not work. Air velocity is greater downwind of a small opening than a large one, so creating smaller openings windward and larger ones leeward is most effective. Windows, sliding doors, screen doors, louvers, wall vents, and other devices can be used to let air in and out of the house.

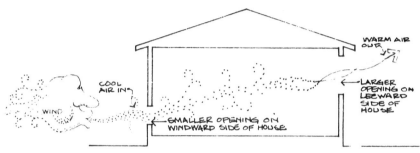

SECTION - CROSS VENTILATION

Advantages/Disadvantages Creating additional openings for ventilation can increase views and accessibility from interior spaces, and can increase natural lighting. Locations must be carefully chosen to avoid reducing privacy and to prevent noise and dust from entering the house. The building must be checked before making openings in the structure. You may have to rearrange furniture to fit new openings.

House and Site Requirements

- Adequate structural strength to accommodate openings
- Availability of breezes on windward side

Cost

Do-it-yourself	$25 and up
Contractor Installed	$50 and up

Energy Savings

Difficult to assess, but natural comfort will be increased

19. VERTICAL AIR CIRCULATION

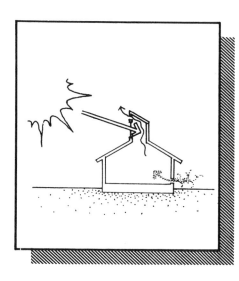

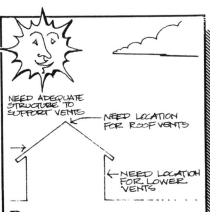

NEED ADEQUATE STRUCTURE TO SUPPORT VENTS

NEED LOCATION FOR ROOF VENTS

NEED LOCATION FOR LOWER VENTS

Resources

• *Design with Climate.* Victor Olgyay, Princeton, NJ: Princeton University Press, 1963.
• *Hawaii Home Energy Book.* Jim Pearson, Honolulu, HI: The University Press of Hawaii and The Research Corporation of the University of Hawaii, 1978.

How it Works Air in a house warmed by the sun, cooking, bodies, and other sources tends to collect at the tops of rooms and in attic spaces. If openings are created to let this hot air out and to replace it from below with cooler air, interior spaces will be cooler and the occupants more comfortable. This can be done by creating openings in the roof, using turbine vents, ridge vents, ventilating skylights, or other similar devices, and creating corresponding openings in ceilings to allow air to escape. Louver windows, floor vents, and other devices can be installed at or near floors to allow cooler air to enter and replace escaping warm air. *Solar chimneys,* glazed boxes similar to solar collectors but mounted vertically and open on the ends, can induce convection currents in spaces where ceilings are too low for adequate air movement.

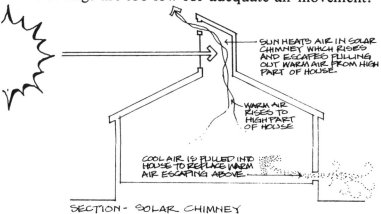

SUN HEATS AIR IN SOLAR CHIMNEY WHICH RISES AND ESCAPES PULLING OUT WARM AIR FROM HIGH PART OF HOUSE.

WARM AIR RISES TO HIGH PART OF HOUSE

COOL AIR IS PULLED INTO HOUSE TO REPLACE WARM AIR ESCAPING ABOVE.

SECTION - SOLAR CHIMNEY

Advantages/Disadvantages Natural convection can be made to work without fans, thus using no electricity. Ventilators can also provide daylighting and allow odors and stale air to escape. However, if openings are not carefully located, dust and noise may enter the house. Care should be taken to keep rainwater out. House structure should be considered when cutting holes, and roofing may need to be patched. Most ventilators will not decrease visual privacy. Fires may spread more quickly with vertical air circulation, so smoke detectors should always be installed.

House and Site Requirements

• Structural check
• Possibility of creating openings

Cost

Do-it-yourself	$20 to $400
Contractor Installed	$50 to $800

Energy Savings

Difficult to assess, but natural comfort will be increased

CHAPTER 6

DESIGN

You have examined your house and you may have decided on solar improvements that make sense for you. Now you come to a basic question: "What kind of design assistance do I need?"

Preparing to deal intelligently with a solar designer is worthwhile for almost any homeowner. Even if you have the skills and are resolved to do the entire design yourself, you will probably want to consult someone with professional expertise at some point simply as a check on your own work. At the other extreme, if you have no interest in doing your own design and intend from the first to hire someone else to do it, you will be more likely to have a design which pleases you if you become educated enough about the subject to actively assist your designer. The key to most projects is a good relationship between homeowner and designer.

This chapter will help you to

• Assess your abilities

• Find design assistance

• Work with your designer

ASSESSING YOUR ABILITIES

If you are interested in designing a solar home improvement yourself, it is time to decide how much you can really handle.

The level of knowledge you will need depends upon the complexity of your project. If you have basic plumbing skills, a simple hot water installation won't be difficult to plan. But if you are considering an active space heating system, you may need technical proficiency with electrical systems, sheet metal, and carpentry. If you are thinking of a structural addition to your house for passive space heating or cooling, you will probably need certain architecture-related skills. It would be unwise to plunge into a solar design until you are reasonably certain that you have mastered the necessary skills.

Novices frequently attempt a shortcut by using ready-made sets of plans. Be cautious of this approach. Every house and every solar improvement present unique circumstances; standardized plans should be carefully adapted to meet your specific needs.

Even if you plan to design the entire improvement yourself, you might well benefit from having a professional check your work. Think of this as a form of insurance. There might be a fundamental mistake in your design. Even more likely, there might be seemingly insignificant areas where small changes could result in greater efficiency. Areas in which a specialist's advice may well prove helpful include sizing the storage system, making sure that insulation is adequate, designing control systems for active solar applications, checking stresses on roofs or structural ceiling members, and designing for ease of maintenance in the event of leaks or other problems.

But there is something else you can do, something so obvious that it is overlooked with painful frequency: talk to people. However many books you read, nothing will replace direct contact with those who have practical experience. If there are solar installations in the area that look good to you, visit them. Find out who has expertise in solar design or engineering and ask them to discuss their subject with you.

Retailers are another source of information you shouldn't overlook, particularly if you will be buying equipment. A good retailer may be able to help you with your design or at least steer you in the right direction. You should always be aware, of course, that a retailer will probably be biased in favor of his or her products.

FINDING DESIGN ASSISTANCE

There are a number of places to look for assistance. You might get the help you need from an architect, an engineer, a designer specializing in solar energy, a community organization offering solar consultation or workshops, or a well-informed retailer.

First you need to be aware of the kinds of services these different sources can offer. An engineer can provide detailed technical assessment and calculations. You might go to an engineer for help in determining the proper size for your storage unit, for instance, or to predict the performance of materials. An architect (or an unregistered designer, who might be just as good for your purposes) would probably be most helpful if you are planning actual additions to your house. A retailer may be able to give you good advice on solar energy hardware. Don't overlook your local solar energy association. They may be able to help you with some or all of these questions.

Once you have determined the type of assistance you need, the next step is to identify several designers. Designers have different styles and areas of expertise. It is important to remember that you are looking for skills to match your particular project.

There are well over a hundred companies throughout Northern New Mexico specializing in solar design, hardware, and construction. One place to start looking for design assistance is in the Yellow Pages under "Solar," "Contractors," "Architects," and "Engineers."

A statewide solar business directory compiled by the Solar Industries Development Corporation is another good place to look. It is available from: SIDC, 300 San Mateo SE, Suite 805, Albuquerque, NM 262-2247.

It's one thing to find a list of solar designers and another to know which one to work with. A good place to start is by asking friends with solar features on their homes. They may be able to recommend the right designer for your needs.

Another place to find out about the quality of a designer's work is to consult the Solar Business Directory compiled by the New Mexico Solar Energy Association (NMSEA) 1372½ Cerrillos Road, Santa Fe, NM 983-2861. This directory contains listings of local solar businesses, the kinds of services they provide, and perhaps most importantly, comments from clients who have used these businesses. The Directory is continually updated. It is available for use by the public at the NMSEA office free of charge, 9-5 weekdays and 12-4 Saturday. (Call before coming on Saturday.)

Once you have narrowed down a list of prospective designers, ask to see their work. Visit projects they have completed, or at least view photographs. This will help you to determine whether the designer's experience covers the kind of work you need and whether the designer's style matches your taste. Check with previous clients about their experiences; it is important to know how the person performs on contracts.

Ask what the designer's experience has been with the components to be used in your project. Solar equipment is continually changing, and you should know if your design will include "firsts" for the designer.

All of this holds true for retailers as well. A good retailer will be able to give you valid information about his or her own products. Beware of exaggerated claims—those who make sweeping assertions about simple gadgets that will meet all your needs no matter what your house is like are not to be trusted.

| Two solar businesses directories are available to help you find a designer. |

WORKING WITH YOUR DESIGNER

The more you know about what you want, the better you will be able to work with your designer so that the improvement will turn out as you expected. Also, if you can provide useful assistance, you may be able to lower your design costs. Sketches of your ideas, drawings of your house, records of your energy use, plus a personal schedule flexible enough that you can work with the designer at the right times, will make the project more efficient.

Think through your priorities as you consider your design. No matter how much responsibility you assign to your designer, you will still be called upon to make decisions concerning costs, level of performance, automated or manual control systems, maintenance requirements, and aesthetic considerations.

However fully you participate, you should also expect the project to go more slowly than originally estimated. Come up with what seems like a reasonable estimate, and then resign yourself to having things take at least twice as long.

One last consideration: establish clearly in advance how much assistance your designer will give you in following through with the project. Whatever type of designer you choose, agree in advance on how much assistance you'll receive with obtaining building permits, dealing with the planning department, coordinating work with contractors, performing site supervision, and checking the improvement once it's installed.

PAYING FOR IT

You should expect to pay for any assistance you get from a designer. You may be billed by the hour, at a rate ranging anywhere from $15 to $50 per hour or more, or you may be billed by the size of the project. In many cases, you can negotiate a fixed fee, which leaves you covered in case unexpected snarls in the project require additional consultation. But as a rule, don't try to skimp on design help that is truly necessary. In the long run, good design is cost-effective and it will ensure that your solar improvement adds to the value of your house.

However the project is billed, you should have a contract or at least a letter of agreement with the designer. A contract should specify what work is to be done, the time schedule for its commencement and completion, the fee, when payments will be made (be sure to reserve a significant portion of the fee for payment only when the job is complete), and any special conditions. There should be a space for both signatures, and you should retain a copy. There are model contracts available at stationery stores. Review more than one, comparing them carefully until you understand exactly what they do for you and for the designer.

Keep careful written records. You should record and date all contacts with the designer, everything that happened, every promise made, and so forth. If everything goes well, you'll have a diary; if problems do come up, you'll be able to make your case accurately.

You should be able to handle these details yourself. However, if you do not feel confident, you may want to contact a lawyer to assist with the contract work.

LEARNING MORE

This is the point at which you should curl up with a few good books, especially if you have thoughts of undertaking your own design. The outpouring of solar books that floods the bookstore and library shelves these days can be overwhelming, but by now you should have a better idea of what you are seeking. In Chapter 5 we suggested some good places to start reading.

RESOURCES

This is also the time to think seriously about attending any workshops where you might be able to gain hands-on construction or design experience. Most solar home improvements aren't conceptually difficult, but in practice they often become complex. You won't have a good idea of the degree of skill required, especially if you are a newcomer to designing, until you move beyond the conceptual stage and see for yourself what is involved.

Low Cost Design Assistance for Owner Builders

Santa Fe —

The New Mexico Solar Energy Association offers inexpensive solar design assistance with discounts to NMSEA members. For more information, call or write NMSEA, P.O. Box 2004, Santa Fe, NM 87501, 983-2861.

The State Energy and Mineral Department Energy Conservation and Management Division offers design assistance to walk in clients. Call 827-5621 for more information.

Albuquerque —
The Design Planning Assistance Center (DPAC) helps community groups and low income individuals from throughout New Mexico with their solar designs. For more information, call or write: DPAC, 120 Yale SE, Albuquerque, NM 87106, 277-3806.

Design assistance is available from several organizations.

Taos —

The Taos Solar Energy Association will help you with your solar plans. Their office is on the Taos Plaza, open 1-5 pm Tuesday through Saturday. For more information, call or write: Taos SEA, P.O. Box 2334, Taos, NM 87571, 758-4051.

Las Vegas —

The San Miguel Solar Energy Association helps owner builders with their solar plans on the third Monday of each month. For more information, call or write: San Miguel SEA, P.O. Box 2634, Las Vegas, NM 87701, 425-5060.

Workshops

The NMSEA offers periodic hands-on workshops and seminars on solar design and construction. Similar workshops are occasionally offered by the Taos, and San Miguel Solar Energy Associations listed above. Other groups offering occasional workshops are: the Albuquerque Solar Energy Association, 801 13th SW, Albuquerque, NM 87102, 842-1531 or 256-3574; the Solar Sustenance Team, P.O. Box 733H, El Rito, 87530, 581-4454; the Ghost Ranch Conference Center, Abiquiu, NM 87510, 685-4333; The Energy and Minerals Department and Western Sun, P.O. Box 2770, Santa Fe 87501, 822-5621; and the New Mexico Solar Energy Institute, Box 3-SOL, Las Cruces, NM 88003, 646-1846.

Classes

Santa Fe

The College of Santa Fe offers night classes in solar theory and design through its Office of Continuing Education, 473-6295.

Espanola

Northern New Mexico Community College offers solar classes through its Continuing Education Office, 753-7141.

Albuquerque

The University of New Mexico offers several solar courses, beginning and advanced, through its Mechanical Engineering Department, 277-2761 and through its Office of Continuing Education, 277-2931. Free solar seminars are given each Saturday at 10 am at the Solar Mart, 134 Vermont NE, Albuquerque NM 87108, 262-2108. The Albuquerque Homebuilders Association offers information and occasional seminars on home solar and conservation measures. Call or write: AHA, P.O. Box 30048, Albuquerque, NM 87190, 265-3509.

Las Vegas

Luna Vocation-Technical Institute offers a solar theory and construction course for county residents. Call or write: Luna Vo-Tech, Camp Luna Site, 87701, 454-0269.

Perhaps a course in solar energy is what you need. One or more may be offered in your area.

CHAPTER 7

BUILDING AND BUYING

Now we come to the nuts and bolts: actually buying or building your solar home improvement. If you're a handyperson, this is the part you've been waiting for. If you're not, this may be the step you've been dreading. But construction shouldn't really be intimidating—not if some good common sense is applied.

This section will help you to

- Decide what kind of construction assistance you need
- Learn where to get additional information
- Purchase equipment wisely
- Learn how to choose and deal with a contractor

DO YOU NEED CONSTRUCTION ASSISTANCE?

Perhaps the first question you should ask is: "How much do I *want* to be involved with the actual construction?" The answer depends not only on a realistic assessment of your skills, but also on your own best guess as to how much pleasure (or how much frustration) you would gain from direct involvement.

How much time do you have? Try to get a good feel for how much work is involved by considering the size, complexity, and difficulty of the solar improvement you've chosen, and by talking with other homeowners who built their own.

Do you have the skills you'll need to do a first-rate job? Those systems using liquids will require plumbing skills, for instance. Virtually any remodeling project involves basic carpentry skills. Have you carefully considered all the details of the installation?

Do you have the money to hire someone to build it for you? The cost indicators in Chapter 5 should give you a rough idea of the probable cost. Providing the labor yourself could reduce the cost significantly. Even if you can't do all the work yourself, you may be able to complete part of the job and save some of the money you would otherwise spend on a contractor.

Be honest with yourself. If you have the time and skill, building all or part of your project can be both satisfying and economical. On the other hand, there's no sense in getting started, spending a fair amount of money on materials and *then* finding out that you're in over your head. Construction mistakes cost money, either in fixing them or in living with them.

If building all or part of the system yourself seems to make sense, go on to the next section, "Building It

The solar business directories described on page 69 will help you find a contractor.

Yourself." If you're pretty sure that you're not interested in that level of involvement, skip ahead to "Construction Services."

BUILDING IT YOURSELF

Your solar addition, particularly if it involves space conditioning, is likely to be a major home improvement, and you will probably need to spend some time preparing yourself for the task. Basically, there are three sources of information for the prospective owner-builder: local solar groups or other agencies with an interest in solar energy; local people, whether homeowners who have done their own building or professionals willing to share some of their knowledge; and publications.

In addition, you may want to seek some practical training in solar home remodeling. Search out workshops and classes, just as you may have already done to gain experience in solar design. And as with designing, you'll want to do a lot of talking to people—both experts and fellow homeowners—to get a solid idea of the practical considerations.

BUYING IT YOURSELF

The owner-builder is faced with the challenge of selecting and purchasing materials and equipment. Fortunately, most of your work will require widely available materials which are used in standard carpentry, plumbing, electrical, and masonry work. You can look in the Yellow Pages for suppliers of these materials.

A Buyers Guide to Solar Energy is available from New Mexico Energy Extension, PO Box 2770, Santa Fe, NM 87501.

For those components in your system which are unique to solar applications, suppliers will be more limited and specialized. If you can find the component you need locally, it's usually a good idea to purchase from the local supplier. If the component isn't available locally, you can either ask a supplier to order it for you or use a solar products catalog to place an order directly.

For some solar applications, kits are available. It is possible that a kit will be appropriate for you, especially if you are planning to install a relatively simple, self-contained system such as a hot water unit. Before you purchase a kit, you need to know exactly what is in it. If at all possible, obtain complete assembly plans first, even if you have to pay for them. Try to obtain consumer information about the performance of solar installations built from the kit you are considering. And as with retailers, beware of kits that promise too much or pretend to offer universal applicability.

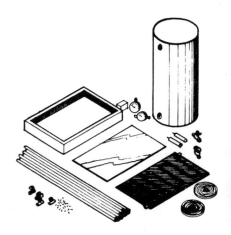

It's worth the extra money to buy the best for your solar improvement. An investment in quality materials will easily repay itself in increased reliability and performance, decreased operation and repair costs, and greater value added to your house.

While shopping, consider both cost and efficiency of the solar energy system. You want to know how much energy will be delivered for the dollars you plan to invest. Take a close look at the components, especially the collectors, and consider these factors:

Durability. How long will it last? Are the materials and workmanship of high quality? Who can fix it? Are parts available? How much maintenance is required?

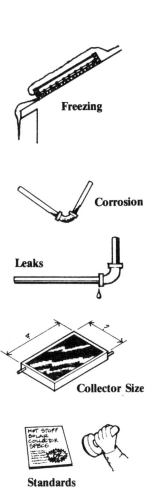

Freezing or overheating. Collectors should have dampers or valves that protect them from temperature extremes. They should operate even if the electricity fails. In liquid systems, does antifreeze solution need to be replaced periodically?

Corrosion in liquid systems. The three metals commonly used in collectors are copper, steel, and aluminum. The safest approach is to use only one type of metal.

Leaks. Leaks are a major source of inefficiency in air systems. The more joints, the greater the possibility of leaks. Know what happens if a leak occurs and how to get it fixed. All joints must be tightly sealed to prevent heat loss.

Collector size. "Rules of thumb" for sizing solar systems ignore many complex factors important for proper design. Make sure a solar professional has checked the size of your collector and heat storage.

Standards. Ask whether the collector meets HUD Intermediate Minimum Property Standards for Solar Heating and Domestic Hot Water Systems, or other industry standards. If the manufacturer claims standards are met, get the claim in writing.

Monitoring. Simple monitoring equipment like thermometers and pressure gauges should be part of the system, so you can check its performance from time to time. An operator's manual should explain how to determine if your system is working.

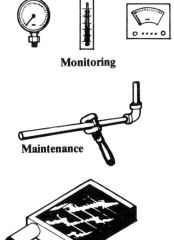

Maintenance. If something fails, who fixes it? Do you need to change the antifreeze fluid, move the collectors, clean the glass, or open and close dampers or vents? Can you shut the system off if something goes wrong?

Insulation. In addition to having a well-insulated house, make sure the collector is protected from heat loss, and that the ducts or pipes and storage containers are well insulated and sealed.

75

THE OWNER-BUILDER

If you've decided to build your solar improvement yourself, you may find these tips helpful.

Plan your construction carefully. Understand what you are going to build and the tasks involved in construction. Determine the most logical sequence of activities, and follow it. Owner-builders tend to start working before thinking the entire project through; this often results in doing work out of sequence because the inexperienced builder understandably completes the simpler and more satisfying tasks first. Instead, break complex tasks down into simple ones so that the work doesn't seem overwhelming—but do things in the most efficient order.

Before you launch a major project, you may find it helpful to tackle a smaller job first. This will give you some practical experience before you start playing for keeps. When you're ready to begin your solar improvement, don't take shortcuts that will cost you time and money in the long run. If you don't have the correct tools or materials, take the trouble to obtain them.

One more note: When you go to obtain the permits you will need, be friendly with your building inspector. If you make the effort to fully understand inspection schedules and requirements and take the time to educate the inspector about what you're doing, with luck you'll gain an ally who will help you avoid mistakes.

Workshops and Classes

The NMSEA offers periodic hands-on construction workshops. Design and construction of greenhouses, Trombe walls, water heaters and other solar applications have been covered in these workshops over the past four years.

The College of Santa Fe offers night courses on solar energy. For information call their Office of Continuing Education, 473-6295.

Solar design and construction workshops are periodically held at the Ghost Ranch Conference Center in Abiquiu, NM 87510 (505) 685-4333 for more information.

The sources of information listed in Chapter Six will also help you in finding assistance in a do-it-yourself construction project or in choosing and hiring a contractor to do the work for you.

Plans

The New Mexico Solar Energy Association sells plans for construction of solar greenhouses, trombe walls, crop dryers, and water heaters. Call or write for further information: P.O. Box 2004, Santa Fe, NM 87501, 983-2861.

CONSTRUCTION SERVICES

Choosing a qualified contractor is a big decision. You're going to pay someone a healthy sum of money to come into your house, work there for a period of time, tear things apart, and probably make a mess. Naturally, you want to be sure that the person who does all this is competent and reliable—but how can you be certain of picking the right contractor?

More often than not, negotiating a contract will be the route you'll choose to take.

The first step is to specify the kind of solar improvement you desire. It's a good idea not to contact a retailer or contractor until *after* you have a basic idea of what you want. The better you can define what you want, the more likely you are to end up with a suitable contract. Describe your proposed project on paper as clearly and objectively as possible and get assistance from an engineer, architect, or designer if necessary.

The second step is to choose several potential contractors. This is the point at which you should identify three or four reputable individuals or firms you feel *could* do the work for you. You want to deal only with contractors you can trust, so the best course is probably not to begin thumbing through the phone book. You might contact some of the groups mentioned earlier. If you've already been through the design process, you probably have another ally—your designer. If you've had a happy experience with a professional in this field, he or she may be your best source for suggestions.

There are a number of ways to find out about contractors. One of the best is to talk with some of their recent customers. Ask the clients if their solar improvements work, if they have had problems, whether the job was done to their satisfaction and on time, and whether they think they made a good investment. Don't count on hearing glowing reports, but do keep an ear out for any serious problems that customers report—such as leaks that weren't fixed, warranties that weren't honored, or work that wasn't completed correctly. Check also with the Better Business Bureau to see if any complaints have been filed against the contractor. You might also check out the contractor's credit rating to make sure the business is financially sound and will be around to honor guarantees (your bank might be able to help you do this).

The third step is to select a contractor who is qualified, has a good reputation, and who has completed projects with which you are pleased. Call the contractor up and invite him or her to make a bid. The contractor will probably want to look over your house and your design, take some measurements, talk with you, and make calculations.

THE CONTRACT

The key to negotiating a contract is to be quite specific about the project. In many ways, this is easy when dealing face-to-face with one contractor who can ask questions and make clear to you what the trade-offs will be (in terms of cost or performance) in selecting one method over another. The value of negotiating is in being able to alter your specifications as the contractor informs you of costs or makes suggestions about better approaches. But before you sign a contract, get your final agreements about specifications down *in writing* and make sure that you and the contractor are in clear agreement.

The contract is the basic document which defines responsibilities—yours and the contractor's. Read carefully any contract provided by the contractor to make sure it protects you as well as the contractor.

A few tips: the contract should require the contractor to "provide" rather than to "build" or "install" a functioning, guaranteed system. This legal technicality ensures that you get both materials and labor for the complete system in case of misunderstanding or dispute. The contract should include a detailed description of the work to be done and should specify the quality of materials, dates construction will begin and end, any performance claims the contractor has made verbally, the total cost of the job, the payment schedule, and who is liable for personal and property damages.

Watch out for these problem areas: blank spaces in the contract document (fill them in or cross them out); vague wording (make sure that everything is clear and not open to differing interpretations); owner responsibilities (be careful of tasks that you will have to perform yourself—do you really want to? can you do them on schedule?); avoidance of liability by the contractor (who is responsible if the system malfunctions and your house or furnishings are damaged?).

Every solar installation should be guaranteed. At a minimum, the contractor should guarantee the workmanship and materials of the entire system for a full year after the work is completed. Specific components of the system may have warranties provided by the manufacturer. Look these over carefully. Be sure you know whether it is a full or limited warranty, and in the latter case, the exact limitations. What is the length of the coverage? Are parts, service, and labor provided under the terms of the agreement? Who provides the service? Do you have to send the component back to the factory for repair, or is it done locally? Who pays for shipping?

A final word of advice about dealing with contractors: *always withhold a reasonable amount of money until all work has been completed*. The entire schedule of payments should be clearly spelled out in the contract, and payments should be linked to observable work progress. A final payment, contingent upon completion of the work, helps to assure a smooth wind-up to the project.

CATALOGS

Solar Products Directory. Solar Age Magazine, Church Hill, Harrisville, New Hampshire 03450.

The Sun Catalogue. Solar Usage Now Inc., Box 306, Bascom, Ohio 44809.

RESOURCES

Low Cost, Energy Efficient Shelter for the Owner and Builder. Eugene Eccli, editor, Emmaus, PA: Rodale Press, 1976.

Designing and Building A Solar House: Your Place in the Sun. Donald Watson, Charlotte, VT: Garden Way Publishing Co., 1977.

The Practical Handbook of Plumbing and Heating. Richard Day, New York: Arco Publishing Co., 1969.

Installation Guidelines for Solar Domestic Hot Water Systems. HUD and DOE, Washington, D.C.: U.S. Government Printing Office, 1979.

Solar Heating and Cooling of Residential Buildings—Sizing, Installation and Operation of Systems. U.S. Department of Commerce, 1977.

By now you should have a pretty clear idea of your best solar options: what improvements fit your house, what kind of design assistance you want, what kind of construction services you need. You should have a basic understanding of the expense involved in making the kind of solar addition you have chosen. You should also know how to obtain a solid estimate or a firm bid.

Now it's time to consider the financing of your solar home improvement. This section will help you to

- Understand and evaluate your financing options
- Obtain the best loan for your needs
- Understand and take advantage of government incentives

FINANCING OPTIONS

The first question you will ask yourself is, "Should I save up and pay cash for the addition, or should I borrow to finance the work now?" Your answer to this question will be based on personal preference and your appraisal of your own circumstances.

The chances are good that you'll choose to take out a loan to cover the costs of your solar addition. If you choose to borrow money, you'll need to understand the kinds of loans available and the sources of these loans.

Broadly speaking, there are three conventional kinds of loans for financing home improvements: mortgage, borrowing from one's life insurance, and short-term.

As a homeowner, you are almost certainly familiar with mortgages. If your first mortgage is of the "open-ended" variety, you can borrow additional funds on it, usually up to the amount of the principal you have already repaid (check with your current lender if you are unsure about the kind of mortgage you now have). With this exception, a first mortgage is usually not the best way to finance a solar addition. If the new interest rate is higher than your existing rate, you end up paying this higher rate on your entire house, not just on your solar addition.

A second mortgage is often a viable means of financing a solar improvement. One of its advantages is the relatively long term of the loan, as compared to standard home improvement loans. Second mortgages entail more risk to the lender and interest rates on them are somewhat higher than on first mortgages. However, since you only borrow

> The New Mexico Solar Loan Fund described on page 85 offers money for solar work at 7% interest.

what you need, the net effect often makes a second mortgage advantageous.

Possibly the best source of financing is to borrow from your life insurance policy, if you have "whole life" insurance. The chief advantage of this option is very low interest rates (the interest rate is printed right on the policy). Generally speaking, most life insurance policies don't accumulate much value until you've had them for ten or fifteen years. To see if this is a viable source of financing for your project, call your insurance agent to find out what your policy's current cash value is.

Short-term loans are often a good type of financing due to their availability. There are several varieties of short-term loans from which to choose: conventional home improvement loans, Title I home improvement loans, and personal or consumer loans.

Conventional home improvement loans are available through banks, savings and loan associations, credit unions, and finance companies. Interest rates vary greatly, and terms of such loans are usually no more than five years.

Title I home improvement loans, created by the Federal Housing Act and backed by the federal government, may offer slightly lower interest rates than conventional home improvement loans. Their chief advantage is a longer term, up to 15 years, which results in lower monthly loan payments. Check with your lender to learn more about these loans.

Personal or consumer loans generally have the shortest term, often no more than two years, and are designed for modest borrowing. Credit unions often have the lowest interest rate on consumer loans.

EVALUATING YOUR OPTIONS

Your next task is to decide which type of loan best fits your needs. Loans vary in the length of time you can borrow money, known as their "term." If monthly cost is important to you, longer terms offering lower monthly payments will be more desirable. However, if total cost is your chief consideration, you are probably better off with a short-term loan which will have higher monthly payments but a lower overall cost.

Loans also vary in the amount of money you can borrow, or their "principal." Using real property as security usually enables you to borrow greater amounts of money. Lenders often place an upper ceiling on the amount you can borrow on a consumer loan. Your financing may be partially determined by the cost of your solar addition.

The third major factor to take into account is the cost of borrowing money, or the "interest." All other things being equal, the lower the interest rate, the more attractive the loan will be.

SHOPPING FOR A LOAN

As we have seen, a variety of loans is available; the trick is to shop carefully for the right one. Obtaining a loan is like buying an appliance—it's worth your time to do a little comparison shopping to get the best deal for your money. After all, loans are the product that lenders have to sell, and some loans will be better buys than others.

The first lender to contact is probably your life insurance agent, if you have whole life insurance. If not, contact the lender who holds your mortgage, if you have one. Find out if you have an open-ended mortgage. Even if the answer is "no," your present lender or bank is still a good place to start, since you already have a history with the institution. Check with your loan officer for the best term, principal, and interest rate available.

But don't stop there. Check around to see what kind of loan another lender will offer. If you belong to a credit union, this will often prove to be the best source for a loan. As a rule, finance companies and retail credit plans offer the most expensive loans, though they usually have the most liberal lending policies.

When you're checking into loan possibilities, dig a little deeper. If the major conditions of the loan seem acceptable, get down to specifics. For instance, you may ask:

- Are there penalties for paying off the loan early (prepayment)?
- Are there loan application fees?
- What happens if you are late with a payment?
- Is any collateral required?
- Does the lender have a good local reputation?
- Do you fully understand all the conditions of the loan? What about the fine print?
- Can you really afford to make the payments?

THE LOAN APPLICATION

That last question, of course, is exactly what the lender is asking about you. The lender is most interested in your ability to repay the loan. Lenders are most comfortable loaning money to those who need it least, so it's in your interest to present the image of a desirable borrower. Be prepared to answer questions about your employment and work history, debt and asset position, banking and loan history, and your credit references. The more stable, responsible, and financially solid you appear to be, the more likely it is that your loan application will be approved.

The lender will also be interested in what you're going to do with the loan, of course. Your lender is going to want to know some specifics about your solar addition, and at this point it would be well to remember that solar energy is still relatively new to some lenders. Be prepared to sell the lender on the value of your solar improvement. In doing so, you may need to answer questions concerning the following:

Design. You should be prepared to demonstrate that your system has been designed in accordance with generally accepted engineering procedures.

Legal. Lenders may want to verify that you have obtained, or plan to obtain, all necessary permits and that the project complies with local building, health, and safety codes. Your lender may require that you protect your access to sunlight.

Business. Some lenders may feel more comfortable about the loan if you are dealing with licensed contractors and have obtained a written warranty or guarantee. Your lender may wish to review any contracts you have prepared. Many lenders may not loan money for "do-it-yourself" improvements.

Economics. The lender will want to be assured that the costs of the solar system are reasonable relative to comparable systems and to annual projected savings. You may show your lender that you can help make loan payments with savings from fuel bills and tax credits. Obviously, the system's lifetime should exceed the loan period.

GOVERNMENT INCENTIVES

Governments at any level can choose to encourage certain types of investments through a variety of incentive programs from tax credits to low interest loans. Current and pending government incentives are listed below but as these programs are continually changing you should check with the NMSEA, 983-2861, the Energy Extension Service hotline 1-800-432-6782, the Energy Conservation and Management Division of the State Energy and Minerals Department, 827-5621, or the Conservation and Renewable Energy Department and Referral Service toll free number 1-800-523-2929 before building your solar project.

TAX CREDITS

The Federal government offers two kinds of energy tax credits. The Energy Conservation Credit allows you to subtract from the tax you owe 15% of the materials and labor costs up to $300 of approved energy conservation measures on your principle residence, whether you own it or are a renter. Items eligible for the conservation credit include insulation, storm windows and doors, caulking, weatherstripping, furnace or flue modifications that reduce fuel consumption, thermostats with automatic setback and energy use meters. The items must be new and you should keep all invoices proving that you purchased them. If the credit owed you is greater than the tax you owe for that year, the remainder will be credited against tax due in following years.

The Federal Renewable Energy Source Credit applies to the material and labor costs of a solar, wind or geothermal system to heat or cool your home or to heat your water. The credit is 40% of the first $10,000 spent, for a maximum of $4,000. Remember, this is not a "deduction" from your taxable income or a "rebate"; it is a credit against your taxes due. For example: if you owe $6,000 in taxes and you have a $1,000 credit from purchasing a $2,500 solar heating system then you will owe $6,000 minus $1,000 or $5,000 in taxes. If the credit owed you is greater than the tax you owe, the remainder will be credited against your taxes in subsequent years until the total amount of your credit is exhausted. (Note that the credit may only apply to your out-of-pocket expenses if part of the system is financed by a special government financed low interest loan such as the New Mexico Solar Loan Fund described below. This policy is intended to prevent "double-dipping," that is, the use of two government subsidies to help finance a single system. This policy may change, so check carefully with the Energy and Minerals Department 827-5621 and the IRS before building your system.)

The Federal Renewable Energy Source Credit supposedly does not apply to passive systems, but there are certain loopholes that have worked in the past. Components that serve a dual purpose do not qualify. Thus, you can't claim the whole cost of a Trombe wall which serves a structural role in addition to providing heat. However, you can claim the purely "solar" portion of the Trombe wall, e.g. the glazing and its framing, the overhang, and the vents. Many people have managed to claim the entire cost of a greenhouse by calling it a "large

Combined state and federal tax credits can reduce the cost of your system by over 60%.

volume air collector" which they claim is an active system since they add a small fan to help distribute the heat. Your local solar energy association may have further tips on wending through the maze of tax regulations. Call the IRS toll free number 1-800-527-3880 for more information on their guidelines and ask for Publication 903 and Form 5695 if you plan to claim either of the Federal credits.

The State of New Mexico offers a tax rebate for solar additions. Retroactive to January of 1981 the rebate covers 25% of the materials and labor costs of a solar heating or cooling system, photovoltaic systems, and wind systems for pumping water or producing electricity. The maximum rebate is $4,000, and you can claim over three consecutive years on more than one system installed on your principle residence or business location, whether you rent or own it.

Passive systems do qualify for this rebate, though those serving a "dual purpose" such as a structural Trombe wall are not eligible for the full credit. For details on how passive systems do qualify, see the July 1980 issue of the NMSEA *Sunpaper* or call the Energy and Minerals Department at 827-5621.

The State also offers an investment tax credit for businesses manufacturing or constructing solar products in New Mexico. For more information see the January 1981 SUNPAPER or call the Energy and Minerals Department at 827-5621.

For information on New Mexico's solar tax credits call the Conservation and Solar Division of the Energy and Minerals Department at 827-5621.

LOANS

A Federal Solar and Conservation Bank to provide low interest loans for conservation and solar work on homes and businesses was proposed during the Carter Administration. At this writing, its status is unclear. For current information contact the Conservation and Renewable Energy Information and Referral Service at 1-800-523-2929.

The New Mexico Solar Loan Fund allows individuals or families with a combined income of under $30,000 to borrow up to $2,500 for a solar installation on their home at 7% interest with five years to repay the loan. The applicant must show that he or she has at hand 25% of the cost of the project and will use it. For further information on eligibility requirements and application procedures contact Chris Perry at the Energy and Minerals Department, 827-5621.

The Farmers Home Administration is another source of loans for weatherization, solar remodeling, and new home construction. They have prototype solar home plans available which are automatically approved for FHA funding. For further details, contact their Espanola office at 753-7129.

There is low interest loan and grant money available in Santa Fe for weatherization and solar remodeling in the form of Community Development Block Grants through the Community Development Program Office in Santa Fe City Hall 982-4471.

Assistance for Low Income People

The Governor's Office of Community Affairs (505) 827-2482 operates a weatherization program for low income seniors and handicapped citizens in New Mexico. They will do up to $1000 worth of weatherization, insulation, furnace maintenance and other energy conservation services on the homes of eligible applicants. They do a small amount of solar remodeling work and also can provide up to $250 of emergency fuel bill assistance.

To find out more about weatherization assistance in your area contact one of the offices listed below.

Albuquerque-Bernalillo EOB
serving Bernalillo and Torrance counties
2010 Bridge, S.W. Albuquerque, NM 87105
766-7221

Sandoval County EOC
1219 Camino Del Pueblo
P.O. Box 757
Bernalillo, NM 87004
867-2212

San Juan County EOC
309 W. Arrington
Farmington, NM 87401
327-9251

Las Vegas GOCA
serving Mora, San Miguel and Colfax counties
P.O. Box 1344
Las Vegas, NM 87701
425-3597

Santa Fe CAO
805 Early St.
Santa Fe, NM 87501
983-7311

Taos County GOCA
P.O. Box FF
Taos, NM 87571
758-4227

PUTTING IT ALL TOGETHER

Let's see how all these incentives work when combined
in a hypothetical example. Gilbert and Juanita Martinez
bought their solar water heater last year for $3,000. They
paid $750 out of pocket and financed the remaining $2250
with a 7% five-year loan from the State Solar Loan Fund.
This year they received their tax credits: $300 from the
federal government (40% of their $750 out-of-pocket
expenses) and $750 from the State (25% of $3,000).

They will pay $44.57 a month for five years, a total of
$2674 over the term of their loan. The total amount of
their investment will be their original cash expense ($750)
plus the loan repayment ($2674), less their tax credits
($1050), or $2374.

The Martinez's figure that their solar water heater
provides 60% of their water heating needs. As they had
been electrically heating their water at 8¢ per kilowatt-hour
that's worth $144 this year, and with the rising cost of
electricity, it will be worth 10% more every year. In the
twentieth year their solar water will produce $968 worth of
hot water. And over the next twenty years their $2374
investment will heat a total of $9072 worth of hot water, a
considerable return.

The numbers in your case may come out differently,
depending on whether you secure a loan or not, what the
interest rate is, what the price of the fuel you're replacing
is, how the price of that fuel will escalate, and many other
factors. In nearly every instance however, a solar
installation will more than pay for itself over the life of the
system. The NMSEA can help you perform a financial
analysis of any solar installation you are considering.

Sunlight may travel freely for 93 million miles, but once it approaches the earth's surface it falls into the same complex legal web that touches every other aspect of our lives.

This chapter will tell you where to anticipate red tape and how to untangle it. Some regulations will help you and some may hinder you, but in either case knowledge of these issues will be helpful. This chapter will help you to

- Protect your access to sunlight
- Negotiate a *solar easement* if necessary
- Understand private land use restrictions in your area
- Meet local zoning and building codes
- Check insurance and warranties

In dealing with local officials on planning, zoning, and safety issues, it is important to remember that many of them have had little experience with solar energy. Consider approaching them with the attitude of helping them to understand what you want to do, rather than pushing them to make a decision in an area which is unfamiliar to them.

ACCESS TO SUNLIGHT

You have determined that your home has access to a certain amount of sunlight. Now you need to insure your access to that sunlight in the future. Basically, you should be concerned with protecting solar access between 9 a.m. and 3 p.m. These are the hours during which most of the useful sunlight will fall on your system.

If your choice is active space or water heating, you may only be concerned with protecting access for your south-facing rooftop or other collector location. If you are considering passive space heating, you should be concerned with protecting access for south-facing walls. Perhaps you plan to use reflectors which drop down in front of your system to increase its efficiency—these also need protection from shadows.

Many factors affect where and when shadows fall on your property. In order to plan your solar home improvement, you studied changes in shadows on your property. Now, to protect that improvement for the future, you need to anticipate changes in the *sources* of those shadows.

There may be no major obstructions to your share of sunlight at present. But look again. Are there nearby trees which are not yet fully grown? Might your neighbor build an addition that would shade your house? Is the land next door zoned to allow new buildings high enough to block

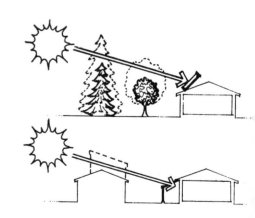

your solar access? Is there vacant land across the way sloped sharply enough that future houses built there would shade your house?

Under common law, you have a right to a limited amount of natural light for interior illumination, but this is not sufficient to guarantee enough direct sunlight for the functioning of your system. However, there are ways to protect your solar access.

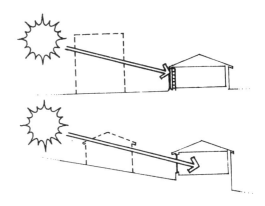

In New Mexico the right to solar access is protected by the New Mexico Solar Rights Act. Basically, this law states that "beneficial use" of solar technologies is protected on a first come first serve basis. The system must heat or cool a building, heat or pump water, generate electricity or provide some form of energy for industrial, commercial or agricultural processes.

Except for a few exceptions (e.g. eminent domain), no one can block your sunlight once you've installed a solar energy system. Your neighbor can't build an addition or allow his or her trees to grow to the point where they will shade an existing system on your property.

That's what the law says; it's never been tested in court. Most communities do not have an established process for recording a Solar Right. In the meantime you should record the existence of your solar installation on your property title and your neighbor's title from the date you receive your building permits.

In various towns, more comprehensive solar access planning is in process. A general solar access policy for Santa Fe is near adoption but technical details still need to be worked out. For more information contact the Urban Policy Board in City Hall at 982-4471.

For more information on solar access policies see the July 1981 SUNPAPER, $2.50 post paid from the NMSEA, P.O. Box 2004, Santa Fe 87501.

Albuquerque has adopted several ordinances regarding solar access and zoning and is the process of developing a solar rights permit system. For more information on how these regulations and procedures affect your plans, contact Robert Romero in the Zoning Enforcement Office of the Albuquerque Code Administration Division at 766-7474 or Box 1293, Albuquerque, NM 87103.

ZONING CODES

At this writing Albuquerque is the only community in New Mexico with solar zoning regulations. As mentioned above however, several communities are developing solar legislation, so be sure to check with your local zoning office before designing or purchasing your system.

In most places, your solar remodeling project will be subject to the same restrictions as any addition to a structure in your neighborhood. Most towns have a wide range of zoning restrictions that vary from area to area. Most zones don't have restrictions which directly effect solar applications, but there are exceptions such as the Santa Fe Historical Zone which restricts the amount of glass on a wall to 40% of the wall area and the maximum size of a pane of glass to 30" by 30". This restriction was not written specifically to limit solar applications, but it certainly does have an impact on them. All buildings within the historical zone must be congruent with the traditional style dominant in the area and must meet approval of the Historical Styles Committee.

Once you have a solar project in mind, go to the local zoning office (in either your city or town hall, or if you live in a rural area the county offices) and present them with a scale drawing of your proposed project. If it meets height, setback, lot coverage, and other requirements for your zone they will give it an OK.

If your system doesn't meet the zoning requirements, you can either redesign it or you can apply for a variance. To apply for a variance you must submit a request to the local Board of Adjustment well in advance of their (usually) monthly meeting. Accompanying this request must be a filing fee, proof of lot of record, and multiple copies of the site plan. In addition you must publish your variance request in the Legals section of the local newspaper, notify all property owners within 100 feet of your property line, and put notices on your property indicating your intent. The Board of Adjustment will rule on your request and notify you of their decision. Solar access policies can simplify this procedure by encouraging solar installations and exempting them from some of these complicated procedures.

BUILDING CODES

Almost any improvement will require that you obtain a building permit and follow the building codes. Building codes protect public health and safety by regulating the manner in which buildings are constructed. They are based on conventional wisdom built up over decades of practical experience. Unfortunately, not too much solar construction took place during recent decades. The result is that solar improvements often fall through the cracks of building codes when they do not actually run afoul of them. It is important to become aware of potential problems in advance. Don't place yourself in the position of trying to persuade a skeptical building official that your solar system is harmless after it is already in place.

Building inspectors will be looking for

- Adequate structural support on the roof
- Adequate rooftop connections
- Safe electrical work
- Safe fire exits from interior rooms if solar additions cover existing windows or doors
- Ventilation
- Safe glazing
- Properly installed pressure valves
- Provision against contamination of potable water by collector fluid
- Proper foundations

To do your own plumbing and electrical work you must obtain a Homeowners Plumbing and Electrical permit. Find out more about this from the Construction and Industries Division of the Commerce and Industry Department, Bataan Memorial Building, Santa Fe 87501, 827-5571.

Most commercial solar equipment is designed with the Uniform Building Code and the Uniform Solar Code in mind. If you plan to build your own, consult the code *before* designing your system. If your design meets code, you will be issued a building permit for a small fee and you're on your way. For more information on this code call your local building inspector at your town, city or county offices.

WARRANTIES

Warranties will be of concern to you if you have purchased equipment, such as a domestic hot water system or components for an active heating system. For passive systems involving structural modifications to your house itself, the crucial factor will be the performance bond your contractor holds.

Be sure you understand clearly what is and is not covered by your warranty. Be sure that you know whether it is a full or limited warranty, and, in the latter case, exactly what the limitations are. Are only certain features and repairs covered? Are parts, service, and labor covered? Are you sure you know who will perform repairs if something goes wrong? Are you sure the parts will be available? Who is responsible for honoring the warranty—the installer, dealer, or manufacturer? What bond or other financial arrangement assures that the warranty will be honored?

In general, a good warranty will include the collector,

piping or ducting, the tank or other storage medium, the pump and other working components (assuming that we are talking about an active system). You should have in writing exactly what you must do to exercise your warranty. You should also know what you must do, if anything, to keep the warranty current. And you should know the approximate cost of repairs not covered by the warranty.

Call the Attorney General's Office at 982-6060 if your warranty is not honored.

There are several courses of action available to you if the business from which you purchased solar hardware or services will not stand by their warranty. Write a letter of complaint to the Attorney General's office with details of your grievance. They will review the case and either take action themselves or advise you on what to do. You can file court action yourself to force compliance with the warranty or rescind the contract. In the latter case, if you can show that the business failed to meet terms or conditions outlined in the contract, the court may rule that you can get your money back.

INSURANCE

Your insurance company will probably consider your solar home improvement as just another type of home heating system or as an addition to the house and will cover your home under the standard policy. There may, of course, be higher premiums to reflect the higher replacement value of your home.

Most insurance companies have had minimal experience with solar improvements, and they may make a point of requiring that the installation meet all local codes; they may even be concerned enough to send a representative to inspect your solar addition. The company may also want to know if there are any potential hazards, such as danger from leakage or particular susceptibility to vandalism, which apply only to a solar improvement. But in general, a properly installed system shouldn't cause you any difficulties with your insurance company.

RESOURCES

The Owner-Builder and the Code. Ken Kern, Ted Kogan, and Rob Thallon, Oakhurst, CA: Owner-Builder Publications, 1976.

Solar Access Law: Protecting Access to Sunlight for Solar Energy Systems. Gail Boyer Hayes, Cambridge, MA: Ballinger Publishing Co., 1979.

Uniform Solar Energy Code 1979 revised edition, available from Construction and Industries Division of the Commerce and Industry Department, Bataan Memorial Building, Santa Fe 87501, 827-5571

92

CHAPTER 10

LIVING IN A SOLAR HOUSE

Now that you're on the path to the sun, what can you expect when you arrive?

Solar energy can be integrated with almost any lifestyle. Perhaps you simply want to save money on energy bills and assure yourself of a steady energy supply. In that case, you may already have chosen a fully automated active heating system, one which, aside from periodic maintenance, won't really have a noticeable effect on your home or lifestyle.

On the other hand, most solar improvements do require a somewhat greater involvement in the day-to-day operation of your house than you may be accustomed to. Depending on the system, you may need to move insulating devices regularly or open and close vents at different times of day. The adjustments you might be called upon to make won't approach the changes experienced in switching to wood heat, a switch that has already been made by millions of American families.

Taking a quick look at the experiences of several local residents who have installed solar improvements may help you to gain a feel for the role that your solar system will play in your life.

Morty Simon wanted an extra room, a place to grow flowers and food, and lower fuel bills. He got all three by adding a solar greenhouse to his two thousand square foot home on Santa Fe's Candelario Street. While Morty had high hopes for the greenhouse, its performance has far surpassed his expectations. Heat from the greenhouse has cut his fuel bill in half despite the fact that three more people live in the house now than did before the greenhouse was built. In fact, the home's three gas space heaters now stand idle as the greenhouse and two woodstoves keep Morty and his housemates plenty warm. Gas is now used solely for heating water and cooking. Further fuel savings have been achieved by wrapping the hot water heater with insulation.

Sunlight enters through vertical south facing glass. Heat is captured and stored in water-filled barrels, a brick floor, the planting bed and massive walls to which the greenhouse is attached. Morty says that it is the most comfortable room in the house. The coldest it has gotten is 56° and that at four in the morning with an outside temperature of 18° after three cloudy days. In summer it's the coolest spot—81° was its high in the scorching summer of 1980 when the mercury topped 100° for weeks

Morty Simon's greenhouse on a winter day.

on end. Three sliding glass door panels in the south face open in summer for ventilation. The large amount of thermal storage absorbs excess summer heat and keeps the space cool and pleasant. Lots of insulation and weatherstripping added to the house when Morty renovated it several years ago contribute to the greenhouse's good performance, helping to keep the heat it generates in the house.

Designed and built by Santa Fe Solar Designs, a local firm specializing in solar construction, the greenhouse cost $3600 in materials and labor. Morty expects to get about 40% of that back in solar tax credits from the state and federal governments. Coupling the tax rebates with his fuel savings, the addition of a comfortable room, and the increase in his property value, Morty feels that the greenhouse was a most valuable investment. **"It's warm and cheerful in there,"** he says, **"people gravitate toward it. It's a wonderful place for kids."** A hammock slung right above the planting beds full of flowers and fresh winter vegetables has become one of the most popular places in the house. As Morty says, "it's like you're in the tropics. It's green all around you and there's a bird feeder right outside the window. You can just lie there and watch the birds."

Since his retirement from the National Park Service in 1976, Tom Ela has done a lot of gardening. For a while he used a small freestanding greenhouse on his patio to start vegetables and flowers early in the spring, and to carry them through the autumn frosts. After a few seasons, he realized that the fan on his greenhouse was running almost continually when the sun was shining, venting excess heat. It occurred to him that by attaching a greenhouse to his home he could take advantage of all that free heat. He visited the New Mexico Solar Energy Association and was assured that he was right. He then had a two hundred and sixty-five square foot greenhouse added to the house that he and his wife Betty had lived in for fifteen years.

photo by Mark Kane

Tom Ela in his solar greenhouse.

96

The Ela's are delighted with the results. Tom claims that the only significant improvement he could imagine would be for the greenhouse to be twice as big. Their home is now warmer in winter, cooler in summer, and their fuel bills are considerably smaller. After the greenhouse was completed, they added a solar heated hot tub to the space. It is now the most pleasant room in the house, verdant with year round fresh vegetables, lush house plants from jades and aloe to orchids, geraniums, and begonias. Tom and Betty read and relax in the greenhouse on many afternoons and often entertain there in the evenings. The humidity from the plants has helped Tom's allergies and the hours spent in the warm room and in the hot tub have relieved his painful arthritis.

Built by Santa Fe Solar Designs, the greenhouse cost about $4,000 before tax credits were claimed, and the Ela's are convinced that it was worth every penny. Considering that it provides additional living space, health benefits, a place to garden all year, comfort, reduced fuel bills, and increased value to their property, Tom and Betty know they got a bargain. While a greenhouse of this type will typically pay for itself in fuel savings alone within ten years, the Ela's aren't too concerned about the finances of the addition. As Tom put's it: "I'm not really sitting here with an adding machine. The greenhouse has simply made this a better place to live, and that's good enough for me."

In addition to the greenhouse, the Ela's home boasts an active solar water heating system. After taking advantage of solar tax credits, the system cost under $2,000 and is now heating a good portion of their water for showers, dishwashing and the hot tub. As conventional fuel costs rise, the solar water heater becomes more and more of a bargain.

Andrée Neumeister's solar greenhouse is more than a source of heat; it's more than a garden; and it's more than a pleasant sun-space where she can relax with a good book. This is a very special greenhouse indeed. For in addition to being a heater, a garden, and a lovely and well-loved room, Ms. Neumeister's greenhouse is her office. She earns her living in it.

Andrée Neumeister is a Rolfer. Rolfing is a deep massage technique developed in the 1930's. Thousands have sworn by it, including Georgia O'Keeffe, Laura Gilpin and Aldous Huxley. Many factors contribute to successful rolfing, but one of the most important is the environment in which it is practised. That's why Andrée Neumeister set up shop in her greenhouse.

Andrée Neumeister in her office.

98

"The greenhouse is a healing space," says Andrée. "People feel better as soon as they walk in." A profusion of green plants keeps humidity and oxygen levels high. This and the warm diffuse light which fills the room make Neumeister's greenhouse a perfect place for massage. "I like to stay in here even when I'm not working," she explains, smiling. "People are drawn to this space, and so are the animals." She nuzzles the cat curled up beside her on the massage table. "There's a rhythm to this room. It makes you more aware, of day and night, the seasons, and of the cycles and forces within yourself. It's peaceful in here. People are impressed by the room's effect on them. They relax immediately. They can't help it."

The greenhouse is relatively small, about eight by fifteen feet, but it heats the entire house through Santa Fe's long winters. Sometimes Andrée builds a fire on cold nights or when she has an early morning client and the greenhouse hasn't warmed up yet, but she's basically free of heating bills.

She's not sure if any of her clients have been impressed enough with her "office" to build themselves a solar greenhouse. What she knows for certain though is that they now believe in the sun's power. There's something almost poetic about the manner in which Andrée Neumeister has integrated solar energy and her healing art. Hers is a perfect example of the benefits to be obtained by opening up to the southern sky, accepting the warmth that is there, and using that gift to restore and warm our lives.

The adaptability of solar energy to the needs and desires of such a wide range of people makes it an attractive technology. Andrée Neumeister, Morty Simon, and Tom and Betty Ela wanted different things from their solar additions. Their financial resources varied, but each found a way to match their needs with effective solar design. Their lives are more comfortable now and they are saving money. At the same time they are reducing their demands on the earth's finite resources.

The first step you should take in readying your house to make use of the sun doesn't involve solar energy at all. As you plan your solar improvement, make sure that your house is adequately insulated and that you are taking every possible step to conserve energy. This appendix will help you to

• Understand the benefits of conservation

• Learn about basic, easy conservation measures

• Find sources of detailed, how-to-do-it information

• Claim tax credits for conservation measures

Effective energy conservation will have a direct impact on any solar energy system you install. Using heat with maximum efficiency will enable you to build a smaller system and, in many cases, a less expensive one. At the same time, a solar energy system operating in a well-insulated house has a much better chance of meeting your expectations. It will also be less expensive to operate and maintain.

Moreover, conservation is clearly in the national interest. We have reached the point at which any new source of power—whether coal, oil, gas, nuclear energy, or even renewable forms such as wind and sun—will cause a significant leap in prices. Yet there are major opportunities for energy conservation; a kilowatt of electricity or gallon of oil saved is as good as a new one generated or imported and is two to 10 times cheaper. About a quarter of our nation's energy use goes to residences, and a large percentage of that is wasted; only about two per cent of American houses are adequately insulated. Effective conservation in the home can play a substantial role in freeing energy for other uses and moderating price increases.

But your personal stake in conservation is just as great. Simple, common-sense steps toward reducing your energy use are not only cost-effective, they are also *cheap.* Many important energy-saving methods cost nothing and others bear modest price tags. Conservation investments pay for themselves rapidly. What is more, basic energy-saving is something that you can do yourself, and do quickly, with no significant impact on your lifestyle or living environment.

Several of the most dramatically effective energy-saving measures are also the cheapest. For starters, you can save a large amount on your heating bill each month by lowering your thermostat a few degrees. Most people are quite comfortable at daytime settings of about 64°F and nighttime settings of 58°F, and houses warmed to these more moderate levels are healthier than those kept at artificial, hothouse temperatures.

Turning down your water heater setting will similarly produce significant energy savings without affecting your lifestyle.

If your gas or oil furnace hasn't been tuned and adjusted recently, or the filter been replaced, have this done right away. Homeowners are often shocked to learn how much of their energy bill pays for a dirty or inefficient furnace.

Common-sense measures like regularly turning off lights and appliances and drawing drapes to reduce heat loss through windows can also make a difference in your energy use.

Caulking, weatherstripping, and treating your doors and windows are very important from an energy-saving standpoint. Survey your house carefully. Look for ragged or missing weatherstripping around doors and windows, cracked caulking around the outside of window frames and door jambs, and cracked or missing putty around window panes. Consider investing in movable insulation for your windows.

In many houses, a very important conservation improvement is attic insulation. If you have an accessible attic, insulating it will be no more than a day's work. There's a moderate expense involved (probably $330 to $450 if you do it yourself), but it's something you can do right away, be done with, and then enjoy reductions in your heating or cooling bill year after year.

Basements and especially open crawl spaces can be insulated; in the latter case, it can be particularly valuable to insulate exposed ducts and pipes. Even poured concrete floors should be insulated around their edges. Hot water tanks should be insulated—this can be done easily either with available kits or with roll or batt insulation.

This is obviously nothing more than a brief survey of the conservation field. Once you have assessed your house for potential energy savings, there are plenty of sources of how-to-do-it information; we suggest some useful ones below. But the key rule of thumb is that a bit of common sense can often cut your energy bill by a third before you ever turn toward the sun for additional heating and cooling.

FEDERAL INCOME TAX CREDITS

There are federal tax credits available for most of the common energy efficiency measures you might want to take. You are allowed an income tax credit of 15 per cent

101

of the first $2000 you spend on approved conservation measures. If you plan to apply for the credit, you should call the Internal Revenue Service and request a copy of Publication 903. This will tell you what measures are applicable and how you apply.

FOR MORE INFORMATION

There are many sources of information and assistance with energy conservation. General advice and information can be obtained through the Energy Extension Service Hotline 1-800-432-6782, Cooperative Extension 471-4711, the gas Company of New Mexico 983-4385 and the Public Service Company of New Mexico 982-4381. Both the Gas Company and PNM will perform free energy analyses on your home and make recommendations regarding weatherization, insulation, and solar remodeling.

As explained in Chapter 8, the Farmers Home Administration, the Santa Fe Community Development Program Office, and the Governor's Office of Community Affairs all offer loans or grants for home energy conservation. The numbers for the county offices providing weatherization assistance throughout the region are listed in Chapter 8.

The Federal Energy Conservation Credit can save you $300.

Active Solar Energy System: A solar device that requires external energy to operate fans or pumps to move heated air, water, or other medium.

Auxiliary System: Conventional space conditioning or water heating system used when the solar energy system is unable to provide all the desired heating or cooling.

Batch Water Heater: A device that uses solar energy to heat a large volume of water without recirculation.

Bearing Angle: The angle in degrees between true south and the point on the horizon directly below the sun. Also known as Azimuth.

Btu: British Thermal Unit, a measure of heat energy. It is the amount of heat required to increase the temperature of one pound of water one degree Fahrenheit (F). Roughly, this is the heat of one kitchen match.

Clerestory: A window placed above the line of the roof to allow sunlight into a room.

Collector, Air: A solar device that heats air between glazing and an absorbing surface for space heating.

Collector Angle: The collector's tilt from horizontal. The optimum angle maximizes the surface area of the collector for solar radiation to strike.

Collector Efficiency: The ratio of heat output from the collector to the solar energy that strikes the collector surface. It is usually expressed as a per cent.

Collector, Flat-Plate: A solar device in which sunlight is converted to heat on a flat surface; air or liquid flows through the collector to remove the heat.

Collector, Trickle-Type: A solar device in which heat transfer takes place as the fluid flows down the face of collector.

Conduction: The movement of heat through materials.

Convection: The flow of heat from a warmer area to a cooler area by the motion of a heated fluid such as air or water.

Degree-day, Cooling: Refers to the severity of an area's summer. For any one day, the number of cooling degree days is the difference between the average temperature for the day and 75°F.

Degree-day, Heating: Refers to the severity of an area's heating season. For any one day, the number of heating degree days is the difference between 65°F and the average temperature for the day.

Diffuse Solar Radiation: Sunlight that is scattered in the sky by clouds and the atmosphere and strikes the earth from a variety of angles.

Direct Gain: Sunlight that enters a house through windows and warms the interior directly.

Drum Wall: A type of thermal storage wall using stacked drums filled with water behind glazing to collect and store heat.

Easement, Solar: A private legal agreement which ensures property direct access to the sun.

Flashing: Thin strip of material used to prevent water seepage through roofs and walls.

Glazing: Transparent or translucent coverings which allow light to enter rooms and solar collectors while providing weather protection. Window glass and clear plastic films are examples of glazing.

Glazing, Double: Two parallel glazing surfaces, usually built to reduce the loss of heat from the structure or collector.

Heat Pump: A device which compresses and expands a refrigerant to absorb and transfer heat from one source to another. Using a reversible cycle, it can heat in the winter and cool in the summer.

Heat Storage: Methods to retain heat when it is abundant for times when it is needed. Usually, it is collected during the daytime for release during the night. Almost all solar devices require storage to be effective.

Indirect Gain: Usually, the use of a thermal storage wall between sunlight and the interior space. Heat is absorbed by the mass and re-radiated into the interior.

Infiltration: The uncontrolled movement of outside air into the house through spaces or cracks around the windows and doors or through cracks in the walls, roof, or floor.

Isolated Gain System: A system in which the solar collector is on the exterior of the house and the collected heat is moved indoors by ducts or pipes. Thus areas not directly available to sunlight obtain heat from the sun.

Insolation: The total solar energy, including direct and indirect, that strikes a surface that is exposed to the sun.

Insulation: A material that resists or retards the flow of heat.

Microclimate: Site-specific conditions which may differ from the general climate due to local topography.

Passive Solar Energy System: A solar heating system that uses no external energy (i.e., for fans or pumps) to move collected heat from the collector to the area where it is to be used.

Retrofit: The application of solar heating or cooling principles, or devices, to existing structures.

Rock Storage System: A system that stores heat in a rock bin for later use. Warm air can be blown through during the day and stored for use at night or during cloudy periods.

Solar Altitude: This is the angle of the sun above the horizon. It is measured vertically and is higher in summer, lower in winter.

Solar Chimney: Vertical space or shaft which uses the heat of the sun to provide upward air circulation for cooling.

Solar Greenhouse: A greenhouse designed to heat itself and, if attached, to provide heat during the winter and cooling during the summer.

Sun Chart: A paper-and-pencil tool for determining solar access. See example in the back of the book.

Therm: A measure of heat energy equal to 100,000 Btu; it is the energy contained in approximately 100 cubic feet of natural gas.

Thermal Mass: Materials that have a high capacity for absorbing heat and change temperature slowly. These materials are used to absorb and retain solar energy. They include water, rocks, masonry, and earth.

Thermal Storage Wall: A glazed wall made of masonry, water, rock, or other materials which is used to collect and store heat from the sun during the daytime for release at night or during cloudy periods.

Thermosiphoning: This is a natural movement of water or other fluids caused by gravity. The lighter warm fluids rise and the heavier cool fluids sink. Using this principle some collectors move fluids without the assistance of pumps.

Transit: A surveying instrument for measuring angles.

Trombe Wall: An external masonry wall of the house that is glazed so that it acts as a collector and heat storage device. A type of thermal storage wall.

Variance: A procedure allowing an individual to build a structure not in conformance with local regulations.

Water Wall: A glazed wall of water-filled containers which receives direct sunlight and acts as both a collector and thermal storage device. A type of thermal storage wall.

Window Box Heater: A small convection solar heating device which is installed under a south facing window.

SIGHT ALONG THIS TOP EDGE

ATTACH A WEIGHTED STRING WITH A PIN OR PAPER CLIP AT THIS POINT.

GLUE THIS SHEET TO A PIECE OF STIFF CARDBOARD WITH THE TOP EDGE ALIGNED WITH THE EDGE OF THE CARDBOARD

← REMOVE SHEET BY CUTTING ALONG DOTTED LINE, OR PHOTOCOPY PAGE

0° 10° 20° 30° 40° 50° 60° 70° 80° 90°

INSTRUCTIONS

1. FIND TRUE SOUTH WITH YOUR COMPASS CORRECTING FOR MAGNETIC DECLINATION.

2. SIGHT THE HORIZON TOWARDS TRUE SOUTH. HAVE A FRIEND READ OFF THE ANGLE SHOWN WHERE THE STRING CROSSES THE SCALE.

3. RECORD HORIZON ANGLE (ALTITUDE) ON THE SUN CHART.

4. SIGHT THE HORIZON AT EACH 15° INCREMENT TO THE EAST OF SOUTH AND RECORD ON THE SUN CHART.

5. SIGHT THE HORIZON AT EACH 15° INCREMENT TO THE WEST OF SOUTH AND RECORD ON THE SUN CHART.

6. CONNECT THE POINTS WITH A LINE. THE SITE WHERE YOU TOOK THE READINGS WILL BE SUNNY AT THE TIME INDICATED ABOVE YOUR LINE ON THE CHART AND SHADED AT THE TIMES BELOW THE LINE.

Reader Response Card

The NMSEA would appreciate your comments on this guide. This will enable us to improve it in subsequent editions. Please clip and return this questionnaire to the address on the other side.

Circle the one number that best represents your answer for each question. Supply other information as requested.

How much will you use solar energy in your home?

Not at all 0   1   2   3   4   5 A great deal

Are you considering solar energy for: ☐ New Construction ☐ Remodel ☐ Selecting a new home

For your purposes, what are the major obstacles to implement solar technology in your home? Explain:

_____

_____

Did this guide help you? Explain: _____

_____

Is guide up to date for your purposes?

Very much so 5   4   3   2   1   0 Not at all

What is your overall reaction to reading the guide?

Struggled through 0   1   2   3   4   5 Enjoyed

What did you like least?_____

What did you like most? _____

What was most useful in the guide? _____

What information was not in the guide that you needed? _____

_____

Did the guide improve decision(s) you made?

Very much 5   4   3   2   1   0 Little

What decision(s) did you make? _____

How much did you learn from the guide?

Not a thing 0   1   2   3   4   5 A great deal

Did you get the guide on recommendation of: ☐ Friend ☐ Professional ☐ Advertisement ☐ Other_____

Received the guide from:
☐ Bookstore   ☐ Solar Energy Business   ☐ Utility
☐ Government Office   ☐ Solar Energy Organization   ☐ Other _____

Date: _____

_____
Name (optional)

_____
No. & Street

_____
City   State   ZIP

New Mexico Solar Energy Association
P.O. Box 2004
Santa Fe, NM 87501

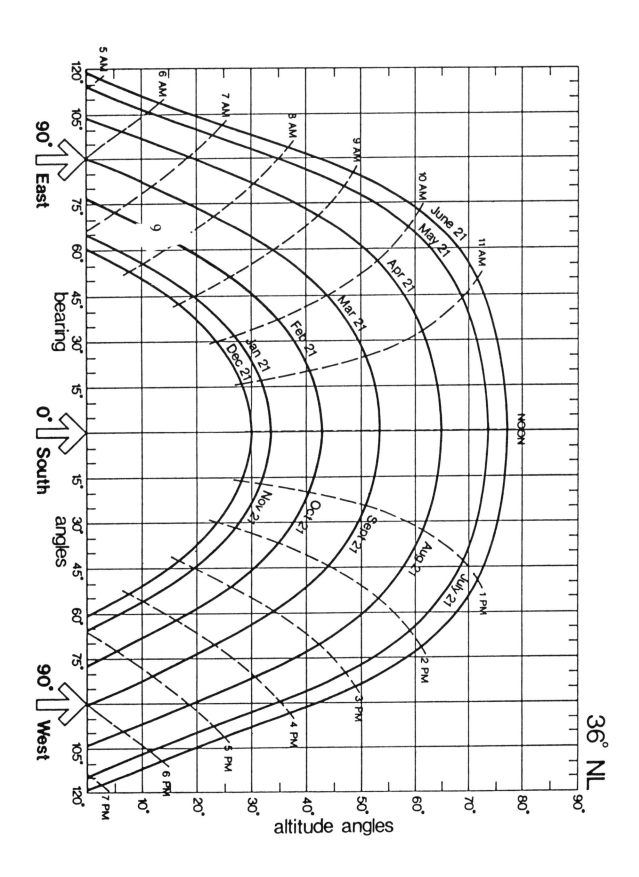

NEW MEXICO SOLAR ENERGY ASSOCIATION PUBLICATIONS

NEWLY REVISED SLIDE SETS ON PASSIVE SOLAR ENERGY

Set A   A general introduction to passive solar applications.
Set B   A look at direct gain applications around the world.
Set C   The use of geometry, shading, and movable insulation in solar design.
Set D   An overview of thermal storage walls.
Set E   Greenhouses in remodeling and new construction.
Set F   Roof ponds and convective loops.

All sets contain 20 slides and a script with explanations of each slide. $12.75 per set ($10.75 for NMSEA members). All six sets (120 slides) $76.50 ($64.50 for NMSEA members). American currency please. Prices are post paid. Foreign orders please add 10%. Allow 4-6 weeks for delivery. A cassette tape presentation by Dr. J. Douglas Balcomb is available as a complement to these slides for an additional $5.

BUILDING YOUR SOLAR GREENHOUSE

Detailed construction plans and accompanying text guide even the novice builder through the construction of a solar greenhouse. 80 pp. $6.95 ppd ($5.75 members).

THERMAL STORAGE WALL DESIGN MANUAL

A complete guide to the design and construction of Trombe walls, drum walls, and water filled masonry walls. Includes valuable information on retrofits. Being used by several architecture schools as a required text. 50 pp. $4.75 ppd. ($3.95 members).

WINDOW MOUNTED SOLAR COLLECTOR

Construction details for building your own window box collector. 9 pp. $1.75 ppd. ($1.55 members).

CROP DRYER MANUAL

Enjoy naturally preserved fruits, vegetables and herbs year round. Detailed plans for constructing your own low-cost solar crop dryer. 12 pp. $2.25 ppd. ($1.95 members).

ORDER FORM

QUANTITY	TITLE	UNIT PRICE	AMOUNT
_____	WINDOW MOUNTED SOLAR COLLECTOR	1.75 (1.55)	_____
_____	CROP DRYER MANUAL	2.25 (1.95)	_____
_____	THERMAL STORAGE WALL MANUAL	4.75 (3.95)	_____
_____	BUILDING YOUR SOLAR GREENHOUSE	6.95 (5.75)	_____
_____	SLIDE SETS □ A □ B □ C □ D □ E □ F	Tape prices above	_____

Name _____

Address _____

City _____ State _____ Zip _____

110